SUCCESS ON THE LINE

The ABC's of Telephone Selling

Martin M. Novich

SUCCESS
ON THE
LINE

SUCCESS ON THE LINE

The ABC's of Telephone Selling

Martin M. Novich

amacom

American Management Association

Library of Congress Cataloging-in-Publication Data

Novich, Martin M.
    Success on the line : the ABC's of telephone selling / Martin M. Novich.
        p. cm.
    Includes index.
    ISBN 0-8144-7725-9
    1. Telephone selling. I. Title.
HF5438.3.N68 1989
658.8'4—dc20

HF
5438.3
N68
1989

89-45454
CIP

Printing number

10 9 8 7 6 5 4 3 2 1

To the late Jules Perleman, M.D.
and
To my son, Ivan Ross Novich,
for his devotion and his confidence in me.
He is a true champion!

CONTENTS

FOREWORD

The book you are holding represents the accumulated knowledge of a man involved in sales management and training for more than ten years. But it is not just another collection of "how-to" homilies by an old-timer; it represents Martin Novich's views on salesmanship principles and telemarketing techniques as they have evolved.

Most books on sales rely on some very basic, over-used ideas. But Mr. Novich brings a fresh outlook, coupled with intensive research into the latest selling methodologies. The result is something new—a salesmanship writer who takes advantage of the lessons of the past while keeping his gaze fixed firmly on the future.

The many people who have read Mr. Novich's magazine articles will be pleased to know that this book contains all-new information incorporating the most up-to-date sales techniques available. Both veteran salespeople and newcomers to the field will find much that relates directly to their work.

So sit back, relax, and get ready to enjoy this outstanding book. And get ready to absorb some information that will be vital to the health of your sales career. This book is virtually certain to improve any sales professional's profit margin.

Robert Rawls
Editor, *Selling Direct*

ACKNOWLEDGMENTS

It has been my dream for many years to write this book on telemarketing, if for no other reason than to honor the salespeople who worked under my supervision. Without those people to observe, I myself would not have learned.

But there are others with whom discussions on my ideas led to deeper explanations and solutions to telephone selling problems.

First among the people who motivated me intellectually and expanded my emotional capacity was Esta Livingston.

My longtime friend, Larry Greenfield, whose faith in me and my work showed no limits.

Bill Abbott, my immediate supervisor for nine years and a great friend.

Professor Paul Violi, my instructor in writing at New York University, who said to me quite innocently one day, "Why don't you write a book?"

Looking back to my life prior to meeting the people I mentioned, there was so little support for my ambitions that I owe these four people more than I can express in words.

The typist, Cynthia Berkey, who did the final draft, must be congratulated for reading my scratchy handwriting.

Pete Ferguson and Dan Oyewale contributed time and other efforts to the book's successful completion.

To the others who helped me conceive ideas for this book, Leonard Smiley, Cathy Carpini, Tina Winfield, Dotty Cohen, Yetta Nemerson, and Frank Mazza, as well as my two older children, Steve and Cara, I thank you. A special thank you to Larry "Ratzo" Sloman, Ed Subinsky, Jim Cusmano, and Richard Tambor. The former three are great screen and book writers who contributed their efforts to *Animal House* and *European Vacation*. The latter, Richard Tambor, helped me put on the finishing touches and contributed his time, effort, and wonderfully creative ideas about telephone selling.

My nostalgia and good feeling make it mandatory that I thank Joan Bressler, wherever you are, for showing me I was special early on in my life.

A very special thank you goes to Marilyn Bush Leleiko.

And my deep gratitude to my maternal grandmother, Esta Bach, for giving me the essence I retain in a crazy world!

Introduction

COSTS =
BENEFITS
= HAPPINESS

The world has changed rapidly since I began to sell by telephone. The overriding fact is the majority of Americans do not have any faith in the government's ability to hold back inflation. Deferring a purchase while money or savings were accumulated to pay for it is no longer as valid as it was while I was growing up, although some people still do things that way. Why do I mention this? Because this kind of consumer psychology opens up an instant market for products and services for the telephone marketeer, and almost insures some degree of success.

In order to bring a telephone sale to a successful conclusion, the salesperson must be cognizant that there is a connection between salesmanship and our social order and economics. It is a compromise in the prospect's mind that has a reward for him, and that reward is called happiness. We as telephone marketeers must learn how to measure the degree of happiness our products or services will bring our prospects in order to close a sale. Happiness and costs are the marriage that can never end in divorce. Certainly there are some prospects who buy anything and accumulate stuff. They, however, are a small minority. Let's face it, buying decisions are in part economic decisions and are not frivolous matters to most people. Therefore, presentations must be carefully constructed and rehearsed. You must be ready for the unexpected. You cannot take the sale for granted. The cold call is the bait on the hook, like trolling in the water, if you will, for the telephone salesperson. Our consumer-oriented society is full of fish, and just like the fish who doesn't even know it's in water, most average Americans don't know that they are urged by media, parents, teachers, friends, and neighbors to buy, buy, buy in all their waking hours.

Consumerism is all around, and this environment creates prospects for various products every minute of every day, twenty-four hours a day. Some prospects will really search out value. Others will be impulse buyers. But all will use the internal measuring device of what makes them happy. This happiness scale is the most unpredictable device there is, for it is individually constructed in every human being.

It starts early in life when a parent asks a child, "Why are you crying?" "I smashed my toy," the child replies. "Ah, ha," the parent may reply sternly, "That toy cost a lot of money. You must be punished." Chances are that child will grow up either of two ways depending on the severity of the punishment—being careless with everything she owns to prove that she is her own person, or being careful with what she purchases. Items purchased by adults could be so constructed that they will wear forever, leading to expensive tastes, or they could be so flimsy that they could be easily broken. As a salesperson, you really don't know what will make that prospect happy at the beginning of the presentation because you don't know him well enough nor are you trained in psychology. So you must ask of the prospect right at the beginning, directly, no matter what the item or service for sale happens to be—what kind of investment will make you happy? What type of insurance policy will make you happy? What kind of theatre tickets do you want? What style of a house did you have in mind?

And now I must interject this question to the reader—What is your fantasy about the rewards of telephone selling? What will make you happy? This last question is not as out of context as it may seem. It is the same as the question I am recommending you ask of the prospect. Do you dream of the commissions you will earn and what you will do with this new-found wealth? A new car perhaps, a new apartment, or a house? Or is your motivation primarily a sense of accomplishment? Close your eyes for a few moments and expand on these thoughts of earning a lot of money. Pretend that you're spending it, or saving it to retire on, or whatever you want to do, whatever will make you happy. Now, open your eyes. You have just found out what the happiness scale is. The happiness scale is pure fantasy.

Because the happiness scale is a fantasy, it is unpredictable. This accounts for a telephone salesperson being almost sure that closing a sale is imminent and then having it suddenly blow up.

Here the prospect's fantasy starts to unravel and many negative possibilities exist. Let us examine the complexities of what could be going on in the prospect's mind. In a general way, this could be true of any prospect. It could be that this purchase would be taking away from a planned vacation or a new car or some other item the salesperson is unaware of. This could be the beginning of a conflict between salesperson and prospect: the salesperson's economic priorities versus the prospect's. The salesperson assumes that once the prospect responds positively to the second call trial close that interest on the prospect's part is profound. The salesperson gathers more confidence about this impending business relationship as the prospect's interest intensifies. Nothing is mentioned about any other interest and suddenly another interest seems to be superseding this impending purchase. The last defensive battle front has been lying there all the time as this very important question comes to the surface or to the prospect's awareness for the first time. If this happens to a telephone salesperson, it reflects true professionalism, for it is a true accomplishment to pry the truth out of a prospect. That question is, "How much do I need the sale item and what do I have to give up to get it?" Since capital and wages limit what a person can spend, that prospect asks: "Is it worth giving up my vacation?" Or the prospect may question the item's value by comparing it to any other item or service previously fantasized about. Herein lies the one and only true objection that the salesperson must ever contend with. Any other objection is superfluous. It is a far truer and deeper form of sales resistance than the salesperson met earlier, for it is based on the reality of life, that of income, restraining the prospect's purchasing power. This fact will always block the fantasy of the prospect having ownership of the product no matter what the need or want.

Certainly if you have credit terms available for your prospect's convenience, it is a great help in closing your sale; but if you have no such financial terms to offer, you must take a new tack of shifting your prospect's financial priorities. Intensifying the need or want is one way, but it is highly manipulative. Nor is it fair to the buyer because it could disrupt business or personal finances. A telephone salesperson must not fall into the trap of fighting for the prospect's dollars openly, for people are reluctant to talk about their income and prefer to infer it in other ways. Showing possessions, such as a new expensive home or cars or clothes which create auras and images of their personal and business success, lets you draw on your own conclusions of their success.

At this point in our attempted close we must turn to the psychology of happiness—back to our original impressions of the prospect's introversion or extroversion from the words and paralanguage used. Our record keeping should have briefed us on our previous conversation and provided information pertaining to the prospect's attitude toward us. Notes tell us how often the prospect was tied up on the phone when we called, and when we did have a conversation, what was the length of time we spoke. Did the prospect make the time for us or was the relationship flimsy to begin with? Were we fooling ourselves all along? What was the free information given us without our asking? What do we know about the prospect's business, hobbies, or golf game? How deeply did you probe about your prospect's business or job? How much free information did you give about yourself? Did you ever decide where this prospect stood on the happiness scale?

If you have carefully constructed a relationship, at this point you can suggest a shift in priorities (as a friend with his best interests at heart), but will it be accepted by him? Another action would be to drop close the sale by cutting the price or your commission or by whatever leeway your employer has given you. A happy compromise might be in order with such a prospect, but if you have relied on your experience and intuitiveness in such a situation, you know how to handle the prospect's last objection.

Training manuals, sales books, and training tapes are reluctant to talk about money or the purchase price of the sale item. We speak of needs and wants with a prospect, but as you proceed in your presentational steps, always be aware that three things are for sale: (1) Your personality in its entirety, including words and feelings expressed in language and paralanguage, (2) the purchase price, and (3) the item itself. You can present the most fluent, articulate presentation there is, and you can always expect the prospect to say at the end, "How much will this cost me?"

DOS AND DON'TS ON COSTS, BENEFITS AND HAPPINESS

DO
Use rising prices as a tool for closing to influence prospects to "buy now" in order to offset yearly inflation.

DON'T
Exaggerate the potential price rise beyond the projected annual inflation rate as stated by the government or an accredited economist's figures.

DO
Be aware that prospects weigh the cost or purchase price of the product or service against the joy or happiness or even the use they will get out of it.

DON'T
Disregard the fact that the prospects' buying habits are based on values taught to them as children.

DO
Ask directly the underlying question of "What will make you happy?" if, after a few closing attempts, the prospect still hesitates to give you an order.

DON'T
Disregard the prospect's fantasies and priorities.

DO
Find out the prospect's fantasies and priorities, but don't belittle them. Compare the fantasy to the cost and the benefits of what you realistically offer.

DON'T
Attempt to compare such things as college education for a child, a family wedding, vacations, or other highly specialized events with your product or service on a priority scale. You will only seem foolish in the prospect's eyes.

DO
Stress the need of your item or service and the enhancement to the quality of life it will provide.

DON'T
Stress credit terms even if they are available to your prospect if your prospect cannot afford the monthly payment.

DO
Take notes about your prospect and use the notes on your prospecting card that you collect to understand your prospect better. The comaraderie that you built up along the way may also be used to close the deal. Trust in you is important!

DON'T
Isolate yourself from the prospect's personal or financial problem. They may be temporary and will be solved in time. Once again, you will have an excellent prospect in the future.

I have seen many a salesperson "freeze up" in presenting costs to the prospect. Suddenly after blurting out the dollar price, the salesperson will then try to validate the price with that of the competition, forgetting the inner happiness scale of the prospect. The salesperson must be aware that he is as much a part of the prospect's happiness scale as the item or service itself. In knowingly purchasing at a higher than usual price that prospect in effect is saying that he is happy with the salesperson. He trusts and he is convinced that this salesperson holds his interests to heart. Unless huge amounts of money are at stake, neither discounts nor haggling over price need be involved. The business deal will stand on the ability of the salesperson to convince the prospect of the service or workmanship involved, or the performance and the integrity of the product. My experience has proven to me that it is never the business deal itself, but the people involved in the deal that are important.

Part One

PREPARING TO SELL BY TELEPHONE

Chapter 1

WHAT IS TELEPHONE SELLING?

Telemarketing began in earnest in 1973, and the growth has been rapid. It is estimated that 10 million people will be selling by telephone by 1990. Many businesses have found telephone sales much more effective than door-to-door canvassing for both the consumer and the business buyer. Increased crime has resulted in laws restricting the licensing of solicitors, which have taken their toll on door-to-door sales. In many areas all sales are now made by telephone.

Telephone selling consists of "meeting" people by voice alone. As a telemarketer I am in a *people* business. To be successful I must understand people. I must be able to "read" their reactions to what I say.

In your quest to improve as a telemarketer you too must start with people. More specifically, you must start as I did, by developing a better understanding of yourself. You will then be able to develop a better understanding of your sales prospects.

I came to telemarketing in middle age, after a long work life that did not involve telemarketing. My education ended with high school. My first telephone sales job was selling chemicals on commission. I found the telephone an exciting instrument for selling, since I could easily reach people who were thousands of miles away. The telephone expanded the reach of my efforts and also the number of calls I could make each day. In field sales, even five or six calls a day is a stretch; by phone I could make fifty or more calls daily.

I was enthusiastic about this job, but I wasn't trained well. I had a good telephone voice, deep and resonant, but had no idea of how to use it. I was always talking. I never listened. My sales prospects never had a chance to digest my sales presentation.

My employer provided a training manual for handling objections, but it was useless to me. None of the answers was applicable. My knowledge of the industry was inadequate, and it showed in the calls I made.

After six nonproductive weeks I gave up. That same day I read a newspaper ad: "TELEPHONE SALESMAN WANTED—We will train you to sell by telephone, draw vs. commission—age no barrier."

I called and got an interview with the vice-president of sales. I was impressed with the orderly hum of the telephone sales room. It had a rhythm that came from the voices of twenty people simultaneously selling on the telephone.

In such an environment, with the support of twenty others, I felt I could be successful. Their voices, techniques, and words would soon mesh with my own. I knew I could succeed with a combination of the sales creativity I was sure I had and the telephone sales presentations I heard all around me.

I got the job and a new world opened up to me. I have found great success in telephone sales. I am now vice-president—of sales for a major commodity brokerage house.

I have learned a lot about telemarketing, and much of it has been self-taught. That is why I know that with the help of this book, you too can find success. All it takes is a willingness to give my methods and techniques the time and energy to work.

The Three Parts of Telephone Selling

Telemarketing is very different from other kinds of selling. It thrives on intimacy and personalization. To communicate freely over the phone is difficult; to sell by phone is even harder.

Successful telephone selling can be divided into three parts.

1. The first is cold calling. How is it done most successfully? What work habits do you need to develop to increase your success? I will explain how to effectively prospect for new customers and how to keep records that will improve your cold-calling efficiency.
2. The second part is the second sales call and trial close. You will learn techniques to help you overcome a prospect's sales resistance and make that prospect an interested potential customer.
3. And the third part is the close. Here you'll learn how to successfully close a sale.

You Can Train Yourself

This book concentrates on these three elements of telemarketing. My emphasis is on how *you* can *train yourself*. Your goal is to close your next sale, and the one after, and the one after that. This book will help.

There is no magic in my training methods, but there is success if you are willing to put in the effort. If you apply my methods and techniques to your own telephone sales calls your telemarketing skills will improve. You will join many others and find success in the booming telemarketing business.

Your training should start, just as mine did, with a portable tape recorder and a telephone voice pick-up. Both are available at any electronics store for under fifty dollars. With these simple devices I was able to teach myself about effective telephone selling. This is how my method worked:

Every morning I placed the tape recorder next to the telephone and attached the telephone voice pick-up. Each phone call I made or received was recorded. Each night I took a few cassettes home and listened to some of my calls. Initially, of course, I thought my voice sounded terrible. Do not worry about this; it happens to everyone. I listened to my sales presentations and the prospect's reactions. I searched for flaws in my presentation. I then used the recorder to try to improve different parts of the presentation. I tried to make my voice more interesting and my language more meaningful.

My method may sound too simple to work. Try it. You will find that if you are diligent, it can work for you as it did for me and for many of the other salespeople I have successfully trained. There are many other ways you can use a simple tape recorder to improve your telephone sales techniques, as you will discover throughout this book. But remember, to improve your techniques you have to do more than just read about my methods. You have to practice them.

To learn the most from this book read it through the first time without stopping. Note any questions that arise in your mind. Then reread each chapter to grasp the answers. They are there for the taking.

Chapter 2

START-UP

Telephone sales are treated by many selling organizations only as a method for getting appointments with prospects. The sale is closed at a later time by field sales representatives.

To this end, both employers and employees have exploited telephone marketing in its lowest form. Telephone sales employment has gained a reputation of offering low pay to solicitors who work to uncover just prospects for others who close the sales. Talented salespeople have therefore looked upon telephone sales jobs as temporary work to get them over hard times. They come and go from telephone soliciting jobs as if they were walking through a turnstile. Good career salespeople are often deterred by this business environment.

But efficient far-sighted telemarketing organizations have shown that a solicitor, if properly trained, can more than justify the cost of the training by gaining more sales for the company.

In selecting a telephone sales position, look for an excellent product or service to sell and good training in product knowledge. The sales room should not be a pressure cooker or a boiler room. That pushes the person's emotional endurance to its limits. The sales quotas should not be set at an outrageously high number of telephone calls per hour or per day.

One young sales manager told me that each of her 10 telephone salespeople must make 100 to 150 calls a day to sell discount telephone services. Production goals are reviewed each week, and if not met, the salesperson is dismissed. In hiring these people, sheer aggressiveness is sought more than a good voice or selling ability.

The average selling life of a telephone solicitor under these conditions is six to eight months. The person's production reaches its limits in that time period, then it slowly wanes because of the pressured atmosphere and the redundancy of the job. It is a case of early burnout.

This type of sales organization holds to the concept of "sink or swim." Just get on the phone and call. Sales training is limited to teaching minimal product knowledge. Marketers are urged to pose as experts. They are called consultants or counselors, even though they have little understanding of the product. No one is called a salesperson; that would be too candid.

A boiler room sales mentality does not look at long-term prospects for a career. Its short sightedness destroys the enthusiasm of all those involved. Sales professionalism is based on ethics and experience and a willingness to wait for what one wants. It is in these two words, "wanting" and "waiting," that we find the basic philosophy of successful telephone selling. You must want to make the investment in canvassing new accounts, but you must also be willing to wait and nurture by recalling those who have been called before. This is the way a telephone salesperson gains new customers.

Hard work is the only formula. A professional in any endeavor works hard for the love of it—income is not a primary concern. The money will roll in when you show concern for both your customers and yourself.

Find a product within an industry that you are deeply interested in, and the task of selling it with good telephone selling techniques becomes easier.

Always remember you are a salesperson. Be proud of it, for it is a noble and true profession.

DOS AND DON'TS OF FINDING A TELEMARKETING SALES POSITION

DO

Think of a tangible product as having its own personality. The product's uses and packaging make up that personality.

Such things as real estate, machinery, and automobiles take on a feature of the alter ego of the salespeople. The same is true of financial services. Introverted salespeople tend to sell more conservative financial instruments than extroverts.

DON'T

Take a job to sell an item you don't believe in; just as you would not choose for a spouse a person you did not believe in. Find a product that you can relate to.

DO

Look for vertical growth potential within the company and ask whether and on what basis promotions are given.

DON'T

Accept employment that does not give any medical support benefits. Aside from the fact that medical insurance benefits are far more costly if paid for on an individual basis than a group plan, they are indicative of a company that cares about its employees.

DO

Check to see how much product knowledge training is given.

DON'T

Accept employment on the first interview. Shop around. Do not look for the highest commission, but the best all round job opportunity.

DO

Check out the company with all or some the following agencies:

- The Better Business Bureau
- The Chamber of Commerce
- The Consumer Fraud Bureau
- The State or City Attorney General's Office

If it is worth it to you, draw a Dun & Bradstreet report. The report will take a few days and there is a nominal charge, but it may be worth it in the long run.

DON'T
Accept employment in a stagnant no-growth industry. Accepting a telemarketing sales position in a growth industry makes it easier to penetrate the market for your share. Prospects are easier to come by and sales are far greater than in a no-growth business. Commissions may be lower in a mainstream enterprise, but volume is far greater, whereas a nonflowing or quiet enterprise may offer higher commissions. Closing prospects for orders may be extremely difficult if the product or service is outmoded.

Moving From Field Sales to Telephone Sales

As the telemarketing industry expands, many field salespeople are turning to telephone sales. If you're one of these people, you know the change from field to telephone sales is a lot harder to accomplish than you expected.

Moving from field sales to telephone sales is difficult—more difficult even than starting a sales career in telephone sales. That's because to successfully adapt to telephone selling, experienced field sales professionals must unlearn some of the skills they've previously learned.

The most obvious difference between field and telephone sales is the telemarketer's lack of visual sense. In field sales a salesperson can elicit a response from a prospect with a smile or gesture, without saying a word. In telephone sales you have only your tone of voice and spoken words. The lack of visual communication works both ways; the telephone salesperson can't see the prospect's responsive smile or gesture either. This frequently leaves the new telephone salesperson without the ego stimulation received in field sales.

The field-salesperson-turned-telemarketer must adjust to this telephone blindness and learn to communicate effectively by voice alone. This involves an emotional deprivation for some because three senses have been lost. The most obvious, sight, is by far the most important in field sales. But the sense of touch—the old back-slapping routine—and the sense of smell—the scent of colognes— are also not available in telephone sales.

How do you build a relationship with a stranger with only your voice and your words? And what if the prospect is also unfamiliar with buying a product or service over the telephone?

There's an initial psychological block, which I call phantom anxiety. Both the salesperson and the prospect are phantoms to each other, which causes anxiety. This anxiety must be overcome if they are to work together successfully.

To overcome this "phantomization" you must project a physical appearance over the telephone. This sounds impossible but it can be done if certain rules are followed. These rules will allow your physical intangibility to go unnoticed. They will allow your prospect to create a mental picture of you as a concerned and conscientious person.

Before I get to the rules, I want you to remember one other important difference between field and telephone sales. In field sales, you can speak in fragmented sentences, using body language, such as gestures and eye movements, to project the meaning you're trying to convey. But body language isn't available in telephone sales.

This means you must carry your thoughts through to a conclusion. Similarly, never cut your prospect off in mid-sentence. Rude interruptions damage the continuity of your prospect's interest, and that damages your possibility of a successful sale.

Here are some guidelines to follow in your move from field to telephone sales. To be successful, these rules must become a natural part of your technique, so you can call upon them as the situation requires:

- Get off to a good start in your conversation—be warm and cordial.
- Choose words that suit your prospect's position and knowledge of the product and/or situation.
- Try not to be facetious. Think before you joke.
- Know your product or service thoroughly so you won't lose your credibility.
- Be responsive to your prospect's questions.
- Don't ramble or take too much time to cover one point in your sales presentation. If you do, you'll find your prospect making excuses to hang up.
- Don't show indifference to anything the prospect says. That can create the impression that you're "above it all."
- Be flexible in your conversation. Be prepared to change direction if it concerns what you're selling, but never change the topic before closing the sale. Small talk can come later.
- Don't impose opinions. By insisting that your views are correct you may get superficial agreement, but you'll lose the order.
- Be considerate. The telephone itself doesn't have a conscience or manners. If your call is an interruption, be courteous enough to say you will call back later. Don't press the conversation when the prospect is otherwise occupied.

Psychological Preparation for Telemarketing

It is necessary for the telephone sales aspirant or the veteran field salesperson moving into telephone sales to understand the internal change that will take place in such a move.

Until recent times, the telephone was viewed as a support system to field reps, to be used as one would use a letter, a postcard, or a courier. Previously, the telephone was used to announce the saleperson's arrival to the buyer, to make appointments, to service deliveries, or to register complaints. It was used to execute tidbits of a sale by both the buyer and the seller. It was not thought of as the instrument to start and complete the sale.

Suddenly, a salesperson is faced with the reality of starting and completing the sale with only the telephone. Such a change can cause distortions in thinking, motivation, and feelings. A good salesman is a sensitive individual, intelligent, empathetic, and compassionate. Practicing your voice inflections and establishing a tone to project one's intelligence, feelings, and empathy is probably the most important prerequisite to telephone selling.

DOS AND DON'TS ABOUT PERSONAL PSYCHOLOGICAL PREPARATION

DON'T
Set goals for yourself that are unrealistic. Set your first goals at minimum levels.

DO
Increase these goals as you become more experienced and more successful.

DON'T
Make promises about your production to a potential employer or yourself that you cannot keep.

DO
Maintain your own discipline. Good eating habits and rest are essential.

A Short Note About Rejection

A salesperson's stories are always of successful presentations, of sales made and sales to come. Those are the stories that are told and retold. The unspoken understanding, when salespeople meet, is that failure is not a suitable topic of discussion.

Why is this so? Because the basic premise upon which all salespeople function is possibility—specifically, the possibility of closing a sale. As the Danish philosopher Kierkegaard said, "And what wine is so sparkling, what so fragrant, what so intoxicating, as possibility."

A newcomer, meeting experienced salespeople at a meeting or convention and hearing the stories of success, may ask, "If all these people are so successful, why are they here? Why aren't they on their yachts?"

The truth, of course, is that every salesperson experiences rejection and failure. Salespeople try to act as if they never miss a close, but every person in sales, even the most successful, knows rejection. And it can be devastating.

You have to learn to face rejection. Success in sales requires learning to deal with rejection and then getting on with your job.

Salespeople have many ways to avoid facing rejection. One will see a failure to close as a personal affront and will feel hostility toward the former prospect. Another will feel that not getting an order suggests unworthiness as a person. Still another will hold onto the face-saving rationale that the prospect will come back, all the while knowing in truth the rejection was final.

There are many excuses, but underneath them all is a feeling of personal inadequacy. In some cases the feeling of worthlessness is temporary. In others, it is more lasting.

Reaction to rejection can be a positive one. Some salespeople thrive on rejection. They see it as a test of their resiliency and they love the challenge it presents. Others use rejection to focus on their need to improve certain selling skills. They critique their failed close to see what went wrong and what they can do better the next time.

If a failed close leaves you with a feeling of listlessness or prolonged depression, your personality may not be suited to sales. A successful salesperson must understand, emotionally as well as intellectually, that rejection is a part of the job. Make sure rejection stays where it belongs—in your business life, not your personal life. It's sometimes a hard line to draw, but you must separate the two if you're going to be successful.

You won't be able to close each sale, but you can learn from all of your sales experiences, successful or not. When you lose a sale, review the presentation in your mind. Try to figure out what the negative dynamics of the conversation were, and how to overcome them the next time. Ask yourself, "Was there an interest in the product to begin with?" and, if so, "At what point was the sale lost?" Try to remember when the prospect "cooled off." Was it when you mentioned the price? Or the product or service? What was said and how was it said? Find your weaknesses and make changes accordingly.

This process of analyzing failed closes should be a continuing one.

Some people believe they will fail and the rejection they experience is a self-fulfilling prophecy. Others hold out too high an expectation of success at the beginning of their sales career; when they suffer several rejections in a row they come crashing down from their fantasy mountain. These people are locked into childlike emotions. They've been assured, since childhood, that they are the best and will always be loved by everybody. Rejection and failure come as sudden shocks. They are unable to relate to the realities of the world.

DOS AND DON'TS ON REJECTION

DO
Believe in the possibility that you could close each prospect to whom you make a presentation.

DON'T
Believe you have to make up stories in order to stroke your ego or to impress your managers or peers.

DO
Learn from the sales experience of other salespeople.

DON'T
Avoid the feeling of rejection after a failed closing attempt. However, do not dwell on it. Never sacrifice energy and time wastefully over something that is not in your control.

DO
Make your reaction to rejection of your presentation into a positive event. Critique the dialogue and timing so you learn from your mistakes.

DON'T
Be taken in by authors who possess the magic one-liners that "open up prospects to sales presentations," or write about how they "made a million." Chances are they are making a million on teaching bogus methods about how to make a million.

DO
Be a creative salesperson, not just an order taker.

DON'T
Try to be a people-pleaser to offset the possibility of rejection.

DO
Develop a sales technique that fits *your* personality.

DON'T
Let all your anger and frustration hang out at being rejected. In the real world of business, we all take our share of rejection.

DO
Keep your personal life separate. That is the place you gain the emotional support you need to face tomorrow.

High hopes for wealth and happiness are fostered by contemporary sales books, magazines, and cassette tapes, which repeatedly extol selling as the road to riches, but no mention is made of the necessary elements of sales success: empathy, timing, business acumen, and the rest.

A good salesperson doesn't rely on the product alone. Mediocre salespeople look to the company and product line, rather than to themselves, to provide success. They want their products to be a "hot item" so they can just take orders without much effort. They want the company to give them literature, advertising, and other support. Backup is needed, but one must not become totally dependent on it.

Nor does a good salesperson rely solely on personality to make the sale. Good sales technique is a major factor in sales success, and it's one factor you can control or at least improve upon. The other factors in the prospect's buying decision—price, merchandise quality, company reputation—are not within your control. Work on improving what you can improve and you'll find success in sales.

Empathy

Empathy—the intuitive understanding of another person's feelings, thoughts, and experience—is a vital component of the good telephone salesperson. Empathy is not sympathy. Don't confuse the two. Simply put, empathy is the ability to put yourself in another person's position.

In sports, empathy allows a player to sense what a teammate or opponent is about to do. In football, for example, the quarterback takes the snap, fades back, and throws the ball far down the field. The wide receiver seems to come out of nowhere, and with a running jump, snares the football. The pass is successful because the receiver and quarterback worked in perfect synchronization and cooperation. Each was willing to risk failure, because each had confidence in the teammate's ability and an intuitive understanding of the thoughts of both teammate and opponents—in other words, empathy.

A successful telephone sales presentation is fundamentally the same. Success requires that you know your prospect and use your empathy to anticipate the thoughts and reactions to your proposition. Empathy allows you to perceive the amount of influence your presentation has given you. It will also help you determine the prospect's interest in the product. Finally, empathy for the prospect's feelings will let you determine the right time to act to close the sale. At that point you must be willing to risk failure to gain success, just as the quarterback must: He can't successfully throw the football without risking an incompleted pass, and you can't successfully close the sale without risking rejection.

If, in your sales presentation, you present the major selling points and facts in an interesting way, you will elicit questions from the prospect as you go along. If you are a good listener, these questions and the prospect's other responses (feedback) will register inside your nervous system. When you sense enough positive feedback, you will literally "feel" that the prospect is having positive thoughts about the product. What you are feeling is empathy.

This empathy will allow you to make a judgment as to the correct time to ask for the order. The time to ask for a commitment is when the prospect's interest is at its height. Empathy will let you know when this time has arrived.

Success in telephone sales requires that you develop your sense of empathy. Refine it, and your timing, by talking to prospects on a daily basis. With a good sense of empathy you will have consistent success in closing sales.

Predictive Empathy

Some telephone scripts have a so-called "predictive empathy" written into them. These scripts are designed to coax a certain type of personality to react positively toward the product or service. In boiler room language these scripts are aimed at "mooches": emotionally immature people; followers, not leaders. After hearing the salesperson's words, the prospect's behavior mirrors the salesperson's behavior. The prospect buys whatever the salesperson is selling. You will receive orders from these prospects, but this isn't the road to real success in telephone sales. For that you need to develop your sense of empathy.

Using Your Time Wisely

Imagine for a moment that you are at your desk and the tools of the telephone salesperson are in place before you: pencils, pens, appointment calendar, a brochure about the product or products you are selling, reference materials such as newspaper clippings on the industry, and most important of all, your prospecting list and your telephone. You are now prepared to earn your living and then some.

A telephone salesperson whose goal is to earn $100,000 per year will need to earn an average of $52 an hour. If the salesperson's goal is $75,000 per year, the hourly average is $39; for $50,000 yearly it is $26 hourly. These numbers demonstrate the importance of the quality of time you spend canvassing and closing sales.

The salesperson is literally an entrepreneur. The salesperson's most valuable asset is time. Unlike the capitalist, no money is invested. There is no overhead with the exception of fare to and from work. Most companies even supply pens, pencils, and pads, as well as prospect lists, and, of course, the telephone. To be successful, the salesperson must properly capitalize on working time.

Stop and think for a moment about the meaning of time. Basically, it is all we have.

DOS AND DON'TS ON THE USE OF YOUR TIME

DO
Determine your monetary needs for your life-style.

DON'T
Give yourself fuzzy answers as to what your personal expenses and goals are.

DO
Be sociable and amenable to your managers and co-workers. You can learn selling techniques from them or they from you, but show good judgment in your relationships with them.

DON'T
Spend an inappropriate amount of time at the water cooler or in coffee klatches when you should be working.

Finding Your Voice

The biggest single reason for failure by a telemarketer is the inability to sell without using body language. In a highly personalized situation the telephone salesperson doesn't have the benefit of a physical self to impress the prospect and can't use the "halo effect" brought on by physical appearance. There's just a faceless voice on the phone. This can be frightening for the new salesperson.

The telephone voice can betray these feelings of anxiety and nervousness. A solicitation by an obviously anxious or nervous salesperson will not result in either a good lead or a closed sale. Nervous people tend to speak too loudly or they hold their receivers too close, spoiling the reception for the listener. A high-pitched voice, a voice that sounds like gravel or the squawk of a duck, or muttering will get nothing but a hang up or at best a "Thank you, I'm not interested." In addition, such a salesperson usually tries to solicit clients at a very rapid rate, running up large phone bills. The salesperson is unconsciously trying to find a person comfortable to talk to. The business purpose of the call has become secondary. The insecure salesperson is primarily looking for an emotional contact—for a transference figure, not a buyer. This is unfair to the company and its budget and harmful to the salesperson.

Voice Tone as a Replacement for Body Language

If your voice is good you won't be just a "faceless voice" on the phone. A prospect who talks to a telephone salesperson with a good voice draws upon that voice to create a mental picture of the salesperson.

With good vocal technique you can effectively project yourself on your telephone sales calls. You won't be faceless. Your voice tones will project concern and conscientiousness, honesty and reliability. This is your telephone personality, which you create through your vocal abilities.

One young woman with no sales experience was hired as a telephone salesperson because of her experience as a member of a community acting group. Through her acting activities she has developed good tones, clear diction, and control of her vocal cords. She now makes over $50,000 a year in telemarketing sales.

Training Your Voice

Voice training is frequently necessary to project an effective telephone personality, but the training needn't be formal. Much can be learned on your own.

Simply read aloud from a newspaper, book, play, or any prepared text that seeks to influence your opinion on a particular subject. Newspaper editorials are wonderful for this purpose. Using a tape recorder, first read the main premise of the chosen material. Pause for a few moments to be sure the author's statement is clear in your mind.

Now, using your own style of speech, read aloud the author's supporting facts. Place special emphasis on the words and phrases you feel the author is using to try to convince you. If you have an accent, don't try to alter it. Accents are helpful; they make you interesting.

Replay the tape to check your tone and diction. Remember, your tone must be serious when it comes to facts. Check also for slurred words. Your words must be understood if they're going to convince. Is your voice scratchy or high-pitched? That will give the wrong image to a prospect. Is your voice a monotone? Your prospect won't develop any interest in what you're saying. If your voice is understandable and also exciting or pleasantly firm, you can count on a good reception.

Have a friend or relative read the same column into a tape recorder. Compare it with your own presentation. In this way you can decide for yourself whether you have an interesting, exciting, and convincing voice, and you can decide what areas need improvement.

Another way to see how your voice compares with others' is to listen to a radio announcer reading a commercial. The announcer is doing just what you will be doing in telephone sales: stating a major premise about a product and then supporting that premise with facts.

The radio announcer's vocal tones set the mood. Once the mood is set, the facts seem more credible and the announcer is more persuasive. If the mood isn't set properly, the supporting facts can seem dull and uninforming.

If you'd like, imitate the announcer. This kind of imitation can be very helpful in learning how to emphasize and enunciate properly.

Singers use many exercises to strengthen their vocal cords and lung power. Their exercises can be helpful to you, too. A singer is a storyteller, putting words to music. A telephone salesperson is also a storyteller. In both cases, pleasant sounds must be produced. One exercise you might try involves holding your breath for an extended time. By doing this (or even by swimming underwater), you can gain endurance and improve your voice resonance. If you're up to it, practicing operatic scales can help you with voice emphasis.

Go back for a moment to the original exercise of reading a newspaper column into your tape recorder. Read the same column to yourself silently. Do you find a similarity between that silent reading and your recording? In both cases you're hearing your own voice, not the voice of the author.

Ask yourself where—on which specific phrases, words, or sentences—you put the emphasis when you read silently. Note these down and replay the tape. Does the emphasis of your inner voice match that of your outer voice? If it does, you have harmony. Your inner and outer voices are coordinated. You can be as convincing to a sales prospect as you were to yourself.

The tape recorder can also help you to establish the correct speed of delivery. One of the biggest adjustments I had to make in calling New York executives was in my delivery speed. My speech was rather slow and laid back. The executives I talked to were very busy. They didn't have the patience to listen to my slow measured speech. Most city people throughout the country are the same. In the suburbs, a slower pace is required.

Many factors affect the prospect's capacity to take in and decipher words. These include geographic location, occupation, and education. The telephone salesperson must learn to "read" the prospect and adjust the vocal delivery accordingly. Remember, many prospects will judge you on the basis of what they hear.

What I have recommended in these simple exercises may not be enough. The practice of reading aloud and into tape recorders or the singer's exercise are all very good if you have a decent speech delivery to begin with, but coaching may be necessary. Speech therapists are listed in almost all urban and suburban telephone directories and should be consulted if you are not satisfied with the results of the simple exercises I have suggested.

The telephone instrument and the lines that connect it from one terminal to another send a *copy* of your voice—not your voice! Your voice and that of your prospect do not transmit the same quality that, for example, the speakers of a hi-fi set do, or even the speakers of the car radio. A poor connection can indeed change the environment, which in turn could alter the sense or meaning of your words. Finally, the way a salesperson sits at the desk or holds the telephone has an effect on the tone of voice.

For these problems a speech therapist should be consulted. And, if you have chosen telephone sales for your career, then by all means do it! It is a small investment to make to earn an above-average income in the future.

Your voice can be trained to sound better. With practice you can improve your voice tones, diction, phrasing, and emphasis. Remember, your voice is your primary tool in telephone selling. A good voice is not genetically determined. Speech therapy or practice and concentration will make a noticeable difference in how you sound.

DOS AND DON'TS ON SPEAKING TO A PROSPECT

DO
Maintain a moderate tone and use inflections in your voice; never speak too loudly or softly.

DON'T
Feel too at ease when talking to a prospect. Examine the reason why: You are possibly being manipulated into a comfortable feeling, taking away your effectiveness.

DO
Take the time to train your voice: tone, enunciation, and proper use of inflection. These are basic to good telephone selling.

DON'T
Be careless in your dialogue. Clearly state everything you think about the product or service for sale.

DO
Seek out a professional voice therapist. Their help could be the difference in whether or not you have a successful tele-marketing career.

Good Listening

Successful telemarketers don't spend all of their time talking. Good listening is a vital part of effective telephone selling. You must discipline yourself to really *listen* to your prospect. That's not as easy as it sounds. People speak at an average rate of 125 words per minute. We think at about three times that rate. It's hard to stay silent and concentrate on what the prospect is saying while our thoughts are racing along.

To be a proficient listener you must be physically up to par and well rested. You must then clear your mind of other thoughts so you can give the prospect the full concentration that's needed.

If you have difficulty concentrating on the prospect, try something that's helped many telemarketers improve their concentration: Close your eyes (or blindfold them) as you listen. This feels awkward at first, but it will help you learn how to listen more attentively. With your eyes closed, you've eliminated all visual distractions. You'll find it easier to focus your attention on the prospect's conversation.

If you still have trouble keeping your thoughts on the prospect, try to anticipate the prospect's conclusion—what exactly is the point of the comments and questions? This will keep your mind from wandering. It will keep the subject matter of the conversation paramount in your mind.

Listen carefully to your prospect's words. They will tell you the goods or services needed, the time problems, and so on.

But don't limit yourself to the words you hear. You must also listen to your prospect's voice for clues as to temperment and personality. These clues will help you determine what kind of sales approach is needed to successfully close the sale.

The prospect is always sending two messages. One is verbal, communicated through language. The second, the underlying message of tone and rhythm, clarifies the verbal message. Understanding this second message is a vital part of your job as a telemarketer.

If the prospect's words are positive, but the tone is negative, you must ask yourself what is really meant.

A good telemarketer listens carefully to "read" the prospect's personality and work with it. Different personalities require different sales approaches.

The rhythm of the prospect's voice will help you distinguish an introvert from an extrovert. The tone will help you determine a passive or an active temperament. "How's your day going?" said in an upbeat manner is outgoing. Said with pauses between each word, "How's ——— your ——— day ——— going?" it may belong to an introverted, anxious, mistrusting person.

In the early 1900s, Carl Jung, the famous psychologist, classified people as either extroverted or introverted. People who use other people to refuel their energies are extroverted; those who prefer solitude are introverted. Most people have qualities of both the introvert and extrovert, but usually one personality type will dominate.

An introvert likes interacting with people as much as an extrovert does. The difference is the introvert's energy is drained by talking; the extrovert's energies are refreshed. That's why it sometimes seems that an extrovert can talk an introvert to death.

When it comes to sales presentations, introverted prospects want and need in-depth explanations. They are usually grounded in reality; facts are trusted. The quality of the product for sale, each nut and bolt, must be described. This prospect wants detail. When you talk with introverts, there will be many prolonged pauses during your presentation. The facts you give are being absorbed.

Extroverted prospects want the same information, but they won't examine it in depth. They will "scan" the details. These prospects trust the salesperson's word. It's much easier to close a sale with an extrovert.

The successful telemarketer must adjust the presentation to the prospect. The prospect won't adjust to you. You must make the necessary changes if the relationship is to work and the sale is to be made.

An extroverted salesperson and prospect draw their energies from each other; they "fuel each other up." Adjustments aren't required.

Changes are necessary if you are extroverted and your prospect is introverted. You must call upon the introverted side of your personality. Realize also it will take much longer for the deal to be consummated and give the prospect detailed information. Similar adjustments must be made if you are introverted and the prospect is extroverted. Without these adjustments you stand little chance of successfully closing the sale.

Knowing a prospect's personality makes resistance easier to penetrate. On your first call, the prospect is acting on intuition. It's the extroverted side of the personality that agrees to accept the free information you offer to send. The introvert will then examine your spec sheets or brochures in detail. The total extrovert will just glance at them.

When you make your second call, the total extrovert will make a decision based on your oral presentation. The introvert will rely on all facets of your presentation—written and oral.

Temperament is also a vital factor in successful telephone sales. If your temperament clashes with the prospect's temperament, it will be almost impossible to sell him anything.

If the salesperson is short on patience and the prospect is slow to understand, it's likely the salesperson won't catch the prospect's signals of interest. Problems will also arise if the salesperson has plenty of patience, but isn't aware of the prospect's impatience.

Listen carefully to your prospects. You will learn to read their personalities and termperments and adjust your sales presentations to their needs. If you don't really listen to them, you will be responding only from your intellect. And that kind of response, without emotional force, is not effective.

If you do try to sell without acknowledging and responding to your prospect's individual personality and temperment—if, say, you follow your sales manual instructions to the letter—you won't connect with your prospect. Rather than listening you'll be mechanically following a script. This may get you a sale here and there, but it's not the route to success. Respect your prospects as individuals and you will be successful.

Blindsight

Though you may not be aware of it, you have a great capacity to sense other people's feelings, even when your only contact is over the telephone. To do this well you must concentrate. Really listen to what your prospect is saying and how he is communicating.

"Blindsight" is the unconscious awareness, or sensory ability, of the blind. But it's not limited to blind people. The unconscious sees in its own way. A blind person can be unconsciously aware of things without being able to see them. And as a telephone salesperson you too can learn more if you allow your unconscious mind to concentrate on what you're hearing. You'll know more about your prospects and their feelings.

When you make a telephone sales call, your mind screens out what it feels is unimportant. You focus on those words that reflect the prospect's interest in your product. But to be effective you must try to learn from everything you hear. Let me give you an example from my own experience.

I got a lead from a newspaper coupon: a twenty-two-year-old man interested in investments. My first thought was that the lead wasn't worth following up, because men that age usually spend their money on cars, clothes, and records. But I made the call anyway. I sensed interest during my presentation, but I wondered about it, since the prospect's profile wasn't right for the product.

When the prospect said "I'll call you after I've decided. I have several propositions I'm looking at," my antennae went up: Was he gathering information for another purpose? Was he a college student collecting information for a course? I don't mind helping students. If I'm asked directly, I refer them to the public relations department for the information needed. But I don't like wasting my time. I don't like to be used.

The prospect sounded older than the age noted on the coupon, but I couldn't be sure. I needed more information, but I didn't want to offend him by questioning his age or his purpose. He could be serious about buying. He might, for instance, have an inheritance, or be an estate trustee. So I said:

Me: You know, I see on the newspaper coupon you sent in that you are twenty-two years old. I have to admire your maturity. If you start buying investments at this age, think what they will be worth by the time you're forty.

Prospect: Well, you see, I was in an automobile accident one year ago, and I received quite a settlement, and I want to put the money somewhere it can grow.

The voice was serious. I imagined the accident scene, my memory bringing to mind a highway accident I had seen a long time before. I became empathetic with the young man.

Me: [*Automatically*] Were you injured?
Prospect: Yes, quite seriously, but I'm recovering now, and I have this little bit of money that makes up in a way for the suffering I went through.

I now knew this prospect was a real one. My blindsight had caused me to say something to the prospect that resulted in my learning of his accident. I let my unconscious mind take over, and it helped me learn more about the prospect.

DOS AND DON'TS ON LISTENING

DO
Always be well rested and physically up to par.

DON'T
Allow yourself to be distracted by side conversations with others while you are on the phone with a prospect.

DO
Anticipate the prospect's conclusion in order to concentrate on the concept of what is being said.

DON'T
Interrupt the prospect—you want participation. Encourage it.

DO
Listen to the prospect's tone of voice. Determine the temperament. Is this person introverted or extroverted?

DON'T

Try to be a bull in a china shop by trying to change your prospect's personal points of view. You must make the adjustment to the prospect's views.

DO

Screen out what is unimportant in what your prospect is saying, but learn about your prospect from everything said.

DON'T

Draw hasty conclusions or form judgments or opinions too quickly. Check them out by asking your prospect directly.

Part Two

COLD CALL SELLING

Chapter 3

INTRODUCTION TO COLD CALL SELLING

Cold Call Phobia

Every successful business needs new customers. That's why at least 50 percent of your working time on the telephone should be spent trying to open new accounts. This is known as cold calling, prospecting or canvassing. I will use the terms interchangeably.

Most applicants for telemarketing jobs express a dislike for cold calling. But, cold calling can help a telephone salesperson achieve a lot. The field salesperson must present her business card to the receptionist and wait patiently to be called into the buyer's office. If she's lucky, her wait won't be too long. The telephone salesperson's worst experience may be to have the prospect hang up or be rude.

Why do so many potential telephone salespeople fall by the wayside? The obvious reason is the salesperson's anxiety at a time when patience is necessary. Impatience arises when an anxious

41

salesperson realizes that a sale may take several calls, spread out over a period of weeks or months. Another factor impairing cold calling is the general fear of failure. A salesperson faces the risk of failure with every call. But so does the field salesperson.

In telephone selling the only way to make a connection is to take a risk. Does the solicited person have an interest in your product or service? Cold calling is an aggressive and ambiguous act, not structured in any sure way to meet the emotional needs of passive personalities. It requires you to push yourself onto others and gain acceptance that way. In a sense, you are crashing the party, not having been invited. But in telephone selling, you acquire acceptance because in business someone who is aggressive and forthright is respected.

I have spent many years wrestling with the problem of motivating people to cold call. Following are some solutions that have worked well:

- Knowing who you are and that your purpose in cold calling is to earn money.
- Make sure your profile list contains *customers:* Remember, the list was chosen because the names on it represent prospects. It is your job to sift through the names until you find the right ones.
- Find someone in the sales room who is a good cold caller. Try to keep up with, and then to surpass, that person.
- Do not set number goals every day. Try to make fifty calls a day of all types: cold calls, second calls, and closings. But this number is not mandatory. Some days you will feel more up to cold calling than others. On a bad day pamper yourself. Go home early. Never be too hard on yourself.
- Allow yourself to dream: Think about the positive results cold calling will bring to you. This is probably the best motivation there is.

Sales and Symbols

Much of sales involves symbolism. Money is the most dominant of symbols. For the salesperson commissions are symbols of success. For the prospect money is a symbol of survival.

At the beginning of a cold call the salesperson's presentation to the prospect is an attack on the prospect's money—and therefore his survival. The prospect cannot survive in today's world without money, but here is a voice on the phone wanting him to spend some of what he works so hard for. The prospect will listen to the cold caller under the right circumstances, but that's all he'll do. Before he spends one nickel he wants to be sure he'll get his money's worth.

We see here the reasoning behind the marketing people's schemes in making sales calls disguised as surveys, free offers, and the like. They are avoiding a frontal attack on the prospect's symbol of survival—his money. They know if they are direct the prospect may become fearful, or even angry, and hang up. But if the voice on the phone has a nice sound and speaks well, if the words are indirect at first, and gradually become more candid, the presentation is not seen as a frontal attack. It's seen as an explanation and is therefore more acceptable.

Fear and anger go together. Both are necessary to man's survival. "Fight or flight" is the classic choice when faced with danger. When a prospect abruptly hangs up on your cold call, he has chosen flight. He is fleeing the danger of a frontal assault on his money.

Making Cold Calls

Physically, it's not too hard to make fifty telephone calls in one day. But cold calling is difficult. It takes a lot of courage to continually invite yourself into someone's home or business in your search for new prospects. You're always facing the possibility of rejection.

At the beginning of a cold calling effort, you may be enthusiastic and full of vigor. As the rejections come along, your voice starts to lose its force and your enthusiasm dissipates. The salesperson's lack of enthusiasm is communicated to the people on the other end of the phone line, leading to more rejection.

I received a cold call in my office late one day. It went like this: "This is Mr. Jones calling to make a free survey on your likes or dislikes of X Magazine." The caller sounded mechanical, flat, and uninteresting. Rather than sparking my interest, the presentation made me annoyed. I thought, "Why should I listen to this?"

To be successful, a cold call must offer the prospect something. At the very least, the call should be made with enthusiasm and positive feeling.

Enthusiasm is essential. It promotes imagery and encourages the prospect's interest. For the prospect the cold call should be like buying a ticket to the movies or the theater. The telephone salesperson should entertain the prospect in a serious manner, while making the sales presentation.

But it's not always easy to remain enthusiastic about the product or service you're selling. One way to retain your enthusiasm is to forget that you're speaking by telephone to the prospect's ear. Do what veteran actors do: Speak to the *eye*. You're trying to get the prospect to visualize what the product or service can do. Speak then to the prospect's eye instead of the ear. To do this well you must visualize the use of the product or service as you speak. This will help you retain your enthusiasm, but only if you believe in what you're selling.

When you speak to the eye you will find yourself speaking in rhythmic tones. Enthusiasm is dotted with exclamation points and upward thrusts in voice tone. When you speak enthusiastically your inflections will rise and fall. Your voice will be more interesting, and you will be more likely to keep the prospect's interest. You may even feel like gesturing. Don't repress your gestures, even though the prospect won't see them. They will help your presentation. The prospect *hears* your gestures, because the act of gesturing gives your voice added rhythm.

The telephone provides the opportunity of direct instant contact with a prospect. But with the instant contact there's a danger as well: The prospect can end the conversation just as quickly as it started and will do just that if it appears the conversation won't be worthwhile.

As the prospector you initiate the call. If the person on the other end of the line rejects your sales presentation and reacts unfavorably to your signals, don't feel like a victim. Feelings of inferiority are uncalled for. And don't become frustrated. Use your energies instead for your next call. Your emotional payoff will come from the good leads you get, not from frustration over the calls that end with rejection.

Remember there hasn't been a cold caller since the telephone was invented who drummed up prospects with a 100 percent success rate, or a 50 percent success rate, or even a 20 percent rate. If you can get one interested prospect out of every ten you call, you'll be very successful.

The main purpose of a cold call is to identify the most interested potential prospects from a list of people. You're trying to sort out the person interested in your product from the crowd.

But the cold call is more than a mechanism to find prospects. It's an important part of your sales presentation because it's the initial step in turning the prospect into a customer. The cold call gives the prospect an overview. Details follow in the printed material you mail to the prospect and in your second phone call.

Because you're trying to sort out interested buyers, cold calling is in many ways a numbers game. You should spend at least 50 percent of your working day looking for the few individuals who will become interested in your product or service. And if the regional or national economy is in a downturn, you'll have to spend more time making more calls. That's why the cold call must be short or you'll never have the time to make enough telephone calls. You need to say only enough for the prospect to react with some interest. One way to ensure that your calls stay short is to use an old-fashioned egg timer. You shouldn't need more than three or four minutes for a cold call when merchandise is involved.

Your calls must be short, but they must also be courteous. Remember you're inviting yourself into someone's home or office. Your call shouldn't annoy anyone.

Think about your own reaction when your phone rings. As the phone breaks your routine you think "I wonder who's calling?" Then, if you're busy with work or relaxing comfortably, you'll probably think "Do I really want to be interrupted?" Even if your answer is no, curiosity or a sense of responsibility will often make you answer the phone.

Therefore, identify yourself immediately. When I get a cold call and the caller introduces himself, my first question is answered. I know who's calling. I will then think to myself "What does this person want?" If the caller's next sentence is "I'm from the ABC Company and I'm selling As," my second question has been answered. I might then think "Should I listen to this? Do I want this interruption? What's in it for me?" The caller's courtesy in answering my first questions, though they weren't verbalized, will help keep me on the phone. And if his tone of voice is pleasant the transition from annoying interruption to some form of interest might occur.

If the call coincides in any way with my needs or wants, I will be much more likely to listen attentively. This factor, of course, is related to your choice of a calling list.

A person receiving a cold call is window shopping, in effect. You are bringing the store window to the shopper and saying, "Please shop with me." Your description of the product allows the prospect to peer into the store window. But your words are intangible. To create something tangible for the prospect/shopper you must send descriptive literature and follow the mailing with a second phone call. That is when you give the prospect more information about the product, attempting to spark deeper interest.

DOS AND DON'TS ON COLD CALLING

DO

Remember cold calling is a search for new business; it is nothing to be afraid of. Without new customers and the business they bring, you cannot achieve personal growth, nor can your company grow. With new business through cold calling you push ahead for both parties.

DON'T

Confront the prospect with the service or product's cost on the cold call. The prospect is concerned with value, therefore, price is not the only consideration. There are other factors that contribute to value which you will explain in future calls to the prospect.

DO

Offer the prospect something, such as "saving money" or "better service." At the very least, offer an interesting personality to talk to.

DON'T
Prospect if you are not enthusiastic.

DO
Speak to the prospect's eye—not ear. You must visualize your product's or service's usage and project it so that your prospect, in turn, will visualize what you describe. This gives the telephone sale a tangible overtone and makes it viable.

DON'T
Think for a moment that you will make a prospect out of everyone you cold call. Turning one name in ten that are called would be an above average figure.

DO
Always identify with the party you are calling. In that way you will discover how to make your cold call interesting. DO ask yourself if you would listen to your voice; is it interesting enough?

DON'T
Make claims about the product that are not true and that you cannot back up.

DO
Describe the highlights and *some* of the benefits of the product, not all or even most of them. In describing some benefits and usage you lay the foundation for the closing call. You will get to know the prospect better on that future call which will give you the advantage of putting your empathy to work. Your purpose on the cold call is to bring the product into sharper focus.

DON'T
Be passive if the prospect says no to your cold call. Use an assertive technique, but don't be rude. You are entitled to know why your prospect has said no. Ask!

DO
Keep a written record of all your calls. They are invaluable in determining the validity of your prospecting list and the effectiveness of your cold calling effort.

DON'T

Just send literature out to a person to make yourself feel good or prove that you are working hard. It is expensive to send information so why waste money or time in mailing to someone with little or no interest?

Literature serves the purpose of making you and the company real. Most prospects, unless specifications are involved, skim the material. Company and product literature serve another purpose on closing calls. There might be an order form or a customer suitability form to be filled out. Highlighting information on spec sheets can be used as reference points in closing the sale. Show care in mailing out this information. Make sure it is for positive purposes.

How to Make an Effective Cold Call

There are two major elements in an effective cold call: (1) the words used and (2) the way those words are communicated.

To deal with the second aspect first, the way you communicate is called "paralanguage." This is defined as the vocal effects, such as tone of voice, that accompany or modify an utterance and that may communicate meaning.

As a telephone salesperson, you use paralanguage every time you speak to a prospect. Your enthusiasm for your product, and your concern for the prospect's wants and needs, are communicated through your paralanguage.

But effective paralanguage is not enough. To be successful, your words and your paralanguage must reinforce each other.

What you say is obviously important. To be effective in cold calling, you must give just enough facts about your product or service to get the prospect interested. The cold call isn't the time to describe all the product's benefits. Save that for the follow-up call.

The following is an example of what *not* to do:

Mr. Prospect, I'm Marty Novich of D.E.F. Insurance Company. I have exciting and unusual material on life insurance that I'd like to send you. I'll use a yellow highlighter to mark the brochure so you can see what it is that I'm so enthusiastic about. That will save your time. May I send It?

What promises have I made? I've said the material is "exciting and unusual." When my prospect receives the material, if he is disappointed—if he doesn't find the material "exciting and unusual"—he will not trust my word. I have started the relationship off with a handicap.

Don't give too much information when you are canvassing products or services that are not of the financial nature. You want to raise questions in the prospect's mind which you will then answer on your follow-up call. The prospect then is a participant, not just a passive receiver of information, and that will help in your close. In successful closing the prospect's participation is vital.

In financial services, give more information and answer more prospect questions because financial services are far more complicated than other products or services. You can therefore give more information initially and still have plenty of ammunition with which to close.

To be successful in telemarketing you must go beyond the abstract word that names your product. You must bring the product into sharp focus so the prospect will become interested and perhaps curious about it.

Let's say you are selling telephones. If you simply tell a prospect you would like to sell her a telephone—"Hello. I'm Marty Novich and I sell telephones"—the prospect is likely to hang up on you. To make a positive response more likely you must differentiate the telephone you are selling from all other telephones. You must bring it into sharper focus. To do this, make your product, the telephone, less abstract and more real: "Hello, I'm Marty Novich and I sell English Bell System telephones, which are the best telephones. Could I send you some information which describes how they're made?" This approach is more likely to result in a positive reaction by the prospect because you've given the prospect something more substantial to think about. She doesn't have to reply entirely on your authority about the quality of the product.

If the prospect still doesn't respond, you can present more facts to uncover more of the reality behind the abstraction "telephone." But don't give the prospect too many facts on a prospecting call. Remember, you will be more successful if you allow the prospect to form some questions you can answer in your follow-up call.

For successful cold calling the right words are vital, but they're not enough. Some prospects may agree right away to the initial mailing of literature, but most people won't. Most will be either somewhat hesitant or completely negative. What do you do then? To be successful you must assertively pursue the conversation. Don't give up at the first negative response. The following is an example of how to use assertiveness properly. Remember to be assertive, not rude. Always keep your voice firm and pleasant.

Salesperson: Good morning, Mr. _____ . I'm _____ of the _____ Company.

[You've now answered the prospect's first question: "I wonder who's calling?"]

Mr. _____, I got your name from *[give source of list]*. I'm calling only those who are qualified for this special situation.

[Now state the proposition, thereby answering the prospect's subliminal questions: "What's in it for me?" and "Why should I listen?" If the prospect's answer is affirmative, check his name and address and make a definite appointment to call back in seven days. Send the literature. If the answer is not affirmative, use the following as examples of how to proceed.]

Prospect: Not interested!
Salesperson: Of course you're not interested! How could you be with the scant information I've given you? That's why I'm sending you this FREE INFORMATION so you can see for yourself what an outstanding OPPORTUNITY this is.

[By mirroring the prospect's last statement you're showing you've listened to his answer, but not understood his reason. This will make him reconsider his response.]

Prospect: I only put money into my business.
Salesperson: You only put money into your business, and that's great!
But when you read my information you might change your
mind about that.

[*Again, you're mirroring the prospect's last statement.*]

Prospect: You're wasting your time.
Salesperson: I'm wasting my time, *but* I believe what I have to offer is
good enough for me to take that chance.

By always mirroring the prospect's sales-resistant phrase, you
give the prospect a chance to reconsider what he has said. If you
refuse to be swayed from your purpose by the prospect's manipulative efforts, you can then proceed with more salient points that
might prove interesting to the prospect or might uncover fears the
prospect wouldn't verbalize initially.

By refusing to let go after the first statement of "not interested"
you are in effect asking for a valid reason for refusal. You are entitled
to one out of common courtesy and you will usually get it if you
are assertive.

The prospect covers a lot of ground with the response, "I'm
not interested." It could mean a lack of money, or he is busy at the
moment of your call, or he buys from a competitor, or his wife
won't let him buy, or he's going through a divorce, or he's joining
the Army. Mirroring his statement might let you find out exactly
what the prospect means by "not interested." With that information, you might be able to turn the prospect's negative response
around to a positive one.

You should mirror other responses also. Whether the prospect
says "not interested" or "not right now" or "I haven't got the money
right now" or "I'm satisfied with the person I'm dealing with" or "I
deal locally," mirror his statements and press on in an assertive, *but
polite*, attempt to get your information across. If nothing else, you
will be remembered for your assertiveness.

Assertiveness is tricky. You must be careful not to cross over the line into rudeness. Try to keep your voice pleasant but firm. Practice by listening to tapes of your own voice. Memorize the dialogue set out in the pages above. Then close your eyes, hold an imaginary receiver to your ears and speak into your tape recorder.

When you're finished listen to the tape. Ask yourself if your tone of voice would be offensive if you were on the receiving end of the conversation. If it alienates you it's likely to alienate your prospects. Experiment until you find the right tone of assertiveness. Remember that tone and use it in your prospecting calls.

If you aren't offensive and proceed in good taste and with courtesy, you will become an effective cold caller.

Chapter 4

PROSPECTING

To make a cold call, you first need a list of people to call! Some telephone salespeople are given lists by their managers. Others must come up with names on their own. If you must find your own names, you can get lists from many sources. Free lists are available, including phone book listings, membership lists, and the like. A local chamber of commerce, for instance, may give you its list of members.

There are also companies that sell lists. Check your local Yellow Pages for the names of these list companies. What kind of information can you expect to get when you buy a list? A good list will of course have accurate phone numbers. But the lists you buy will often have other useful information, such as each person's net worth, and occupation. Other lists will give you information on companies: the name of the executive officer, other executives' names and job titles, and financial information such as yearly salaries.

Selecting the right list for your product is essential. Let the list company's salesperson know what you're selling to obtain the best match for your product. Examine the profile of the prospects on the list. Ask yourself if your product is of use to a prospect meeting this profile. If, say, you're soliciting for a diaper service, you'd want a list of young families. A list of senior citizens would be useless.

Don't make assumptions about your prospects based on their addresses or their accents. You may be prejudiced about certain areas of the country or certain areas of your city based on your prior experiences. But you can't let these prejudices affect your calls. The way to overcome your assumptions is awareness. If you understand how you are prejudging someone, you'll be able to be more objective in your calls.

Pay careful attention to the reception you receive in your initial cold calling. If you find little or no interest in your product or service, the list you're using may be wrong for you. The only way to be sure whether the people on your list have the need, the finances, and the willingness to buy your product or service is by making some calls.

If you're using a list supplied by your manager and you find the list is the wrong one for your product, talk to the manager. Give the facts—ages, finances, needs—to support your belief that the list is wrong for the product.

A good match between product and list will allow you to find interested prospects when you call. It won't guarantee sales, but it will give you a better opportunity for them. If the prospect has a preconditioned need or want that fits your product, your voice will be more likely to stimulate the right kind of imagery in the prospect's mind. Prospecting from the right list is the backbone of telephone sales.

Record Keeping

Effective prospecting requires careful record keeping. Two forms must be used.

The first is the daily call report. As you can see from this sample, it should include the name and phone number of every

Figure 1. *Account executive's daily call report.*

office: _____ account executive: _____ date: _____

time	name	phone	conversation

prospect called and the time called. List only those people to whom you actually speak. If you can't get through because the line is busy or no one answers the phone, don't put the name on the call report. Be sure to note the reasons given by those prospects who aren't interested in your product, as well as any relevant information from calls with interested prospects.

Completed call reports should be reviewed daily and proper mailings sent to interested prospects. Analyze the reasons given by uninterested prospects to gauge the effectiveness of your list and your own cold-calling weaknesses. Check the number of calls made, the number that turn into good prospects, and the number that give you new leads.

A daily call report can help you set personal goals and help motivate you towards better cold calling.

The second important part of your recordkeeping should be a qualifying form for every interested prospect. When you review your daily call reports, fill out a qualifying form for each interested prospect—that is, for each prospect who has agreed to have you call back after receiving your product literature in the mail.

As you can see from the sample, you will have the prospect's name, address, telephone number, and other useful personal data you obtain, as well as a listing of each contact with the prospect, all in one convenient place. You may not get all of the personal information listed, even after several phone calls. Don't worry about it. The primary purpose of the qualifying form is to keep all of your information about a prospect, and a record of your contacts and mailings in one place. Reviewing these forms regularly will help you avoid breaks in the continuity of your follow-up calls. They also will remind you of the details of each conversation so you can personalize your phone calls.

Summarize each conversation or presentation meticulously. It's vital for your success as a telemarketer. You can use symbols such as NAH (not at home), NIO (not in office), OV (on vacation), B (phone line busy), and I (ill) as well as any others which work for you to save some time.

When to Call

You'll be more likely to get a positive response if you call at a favorable time. The best time to call depends upon the individual's

Figure 2. Qualifying form.

Lead Source: _____   Salesperson: _____

Name: _____

Address: _____   Office Tel #: _____

_____   Home Tel #: _____

Marital Status: _____   Age: _____

Soc Sec #: _____   Work: _____

Hobbies: _____

_____

_____

_____

_____

Product Discussed: _____

_____

_____

Bank Name: _____

Information Sent: _____

Notes: _____

_____

_____

occupation. In my experience, if you follow this schedule of best times to call, the odds are you'll have a better chance of being listened to:

Accountants	May 1 to December 31
Attorneys	8:00 A.M. to 8:30 A.M. or after 4 P.M. 5 P.M.
Bankers	Before 8:30 A.M. and after 5 P.M.
Builders	Before 9:00 A.M. and after 5 P.M.
Business Owners	All day long
Clergy	Between Tuesday and Friday
Dentists	Between 8:30 A.M. and 9:30 A.M.
Engineers & Chemists	Between 4:00 P.M. and 5:00 P.M.
Executives	After 10:30 A.M.
Housewives	Midmorning or midafternoon
Manufacturers	All day long
Physicians	Before 9:30 A.M. and after 4:30 P.M.
Retail Merchants	All day long
Sales Managers	Afternoons
Salespersons	Between 9:00 A.M. and 11:00 A.M. or after 5 P.M.
Stock Brokers	Before 9:30 A.M. and after 4:15 P.M.
Educators	After 4:30 P.M. or weekends and holidays

If your prospect is in a meeting or out to lunch when you make your first call, leave your name and the name of your company. Don't leave a phone number for a call back. If the prospect returns your call when you're busy or on another line, the interruption could destroy the mood or rhythm of the presentation you're giving. On the other hand, by simply leaving your name and the name of your company, you are keeping the prospect aware of your presence. He more than likely will be expecting your call later in the day.

DOS AND DON'TS ON USING THE PROSPECT LIST

DO

Make sure all prospecting lists are current and have correct phone numbers.

DON'T

Make any assumptions on a prospect list because you have bad memories of an area or certain group of people. Do not trust your bias or prejudice, only your own ability with people.

DO

Pay careful attention to how your calls are received by at least two dozen people on the prospect list. Spot check the list choosing any names or phone numbers at random. In this way you can tell whether the list has accurate phone numbers and where the people on it possess the right market profile to purchase your wares.

DON'T

Expect a list to get you sales. It will help, but *you* must close the sale. A good list only guarantees you someone to call.

Getting Past the Secretary

The way a secretary screens an executive's calls depends on the protective and nurturing aspects of her personality as well as on the policies set down by the executive. Secretaries, whether male or female, are like parents. I have read about and seen video training tapes featuring all kinds of methods to get past the secretary. Some were devious, others cunning; one plan called for outright bribery. I have found nothing that has proven satisfactory or foolproof.

There isn't a gimmick that will get past the secretary that doesn't either antagonize the secretary or the boss. So I just gave up all the sophisticated plots. To me, "No" from a secretary means exactly that. After explaining the reason for my call, I just take my chances. My canvassing calls go like this:

Visitor: Good morning, is Ms. Prospect in?
Secretary: Who shall I say is calling?
Visitor: Mr. Novich of ICS in New York.
Secretary: What is this pertaining to?
Visitor: It's an investment matter.
Secretary: Oh, I see. . . . She's in a meeting right now. Can I have a number for her to call you back?

The best method for the salesperson to employ when the response from the secretary is "She's on the phone" or "She's in a meeting" is to consider it true. Simply recycle the name and call back later or at a different time on another day.

Don't deliberately mislead the secretary to get to talk to your prospect. Doing this can back fire and harm your sales efforts. If your party is a priority prospect, try a direct mail piece or a personal letter prior to the call, stating the time of your intended call and a brief summary of your offer. Clearly outline the benefits your product provides in the written communication. A legible hand-written note will suffice; in fact, a handwritten note will stand out among regular business correspondence. If you wish send a brochure to accompany the note, highlighting the important benefits of the product or service.

There is one other practical technique: Call before 9:00 A.M. or after 5:00 P.M., when the secretary is not there. The prospect may pick up the phone herself.

Persistence in selling is a marvelous attribute for salespeople, but wasted energy in being persistent is nonproductive.

What to Do When Children Answer

If a child answers the phone, ask to speak to the parent. You can leave a message if the parent isn't in, but be sure to speak to the child as though it were your own child. Children can distort messages—they can even panic their parents with misunderstood messages—so take a few moments to be certain your message is understood. This kind of effort may pay off when you do reach the parent:

> Mrs. Jones, I called yesterday and your daughter answered the phone. I want you to know she is a very intelligent child. Do you know what she asked me?

And go on from there. You'll find the parent delighted to talk with you.

Concluding the Prospecting Call

Be sure to ask the prospect if you might send some information about your product or service and then call again to discuss it. This prior approval is vital. Literature sent without the prospect's okay will take its place in the trash with all the other unsolicited mail the prospect receives.

Finally, your prospecting isn't completed until the printed information about your product or service is sent out to the new prospects you've unearthed. The material you send should include:

- A short, concise history of the company
- Specification or information sheets about the product or service
- A price list
- A list of available models or services
- Your business card
- Any contract or information form that your company requires clients to fill out for record keeping purposes

This information will help you close the sale. Be sure to send it out immediately after your cold call.

Getting Additional Leads

Current satisfied customers are the best source of new leads. Here's how to get those leads and turn them into customers:

Ask your satisfied customers for a handwritten testimonial letter addressed "Dear Friend" and for a list of names and addresses of people who might have some interest in your product or service. Mail the "Dear Friend" letter with any necessary explanatory material, to each person on the list.

Leave enough time for the letters to be received. Then call each person on the list, introduce yourself as a friend of the customer, and move into your sales presentation. You'll find this technique works. Try it.

Don't stop here in your search for good leads. Successful telemarketers can get good leads even from prospects with little interest in the product. Even prospects who say they don't want any literature on your product can provide you with leads that turn into customers. This is how to do it.

When you don't get a positive response to your request to send printed material, don't write the prospect off entirely. Ask the prospect for the name of a friend or relative who might be interested. You'll find that being courteous and not pressing too much with an uninterested person will frequently result in good leads.

Me:	Good morning, Mrs. Jones, I'm Martin Novich of the ABC Company. I got your name from a list of homeowners in Springfield, New Jersey. My company is selling Brand X sewing machines at 30 percent off the list price. I don't know if you've seen our commercial on TV, but it's the same one as advertised. If you're in the market for a new sewing machine, I'd like to mail you some free information and then get back to you in a week or two to see if you have any interest.
Mrs. Jones:	I'm not interested, Mr. Novich.
Me:	Okay, Mrs. Jones, but this offer is going to end in one month. Even though I'm sorry to see you miss this opportunity, is there anyone you know you'd like to do a favor for by giving me their name and number so I can see if they are interested?

This should be done each time a prospect isn't interested in your product. Many of these prospects will give you a lead if you approach them properly. And then, when you call these new leads, use the original prospect to help "introduce" you. As you get leads from other leads, you'll find the leads get stronger. That's because the people whose names you get have a common interest and will feel a lot more trust in you because you come "recommended."

Prospecting for Leads for In-Home Appointments

In some telemarketing jobs your responsibility is to find leads for outside salespersons. They will make in-home visits after you arrange the appointments. This requires two phone calls, (1) a prospecting call, as described above, and (2) a qualifying call, to be sure the appointment will be kept. The qualifying call should be made three to four hours before the time set for the appointment. An example of how this can be done will make the process clear.

Saul North was brilliant in his use of the telephone to prospect for leads to be used by outside salespersons.

Saul's product was home improvements. He resisted the concept of telephone prospecting at first. The way he saw it, door-to-door selling was the most effective method he could use: The salesperson could judge and qualify the prospect and also determine the home improvements needed during a house-to-house canvass. This information was brought back to a closer who would close the sale based on the prospect's needs.

While Saul first rejected the idea of using the telephone to get leads, when he examined the idea more carefully he realized it could work for him. This is how he did it:

First, one field person would scout a neighborhood, setting up useful profiles such as the ages of the houses and the condition of repair.

Then, using a cross-reference telephone book that listed phone numbers by address rather than name, the neighborhood was blanketed with prospecting calls. The initial information gathered by the field person guided the telephone canvassers.

The initial canvass took place between 6:30 P.M. and 7 P.M. The salesperson would try to extract more explicit information about the household and the improvements needed. An appointment would be set up, generally in the evening, for an in-home visit. At 5 P.M. on the day of the appointment, one of the more experienced salespeople would requalify the lead by calling the other spouse. One can find out the best time to reach the other spouse from the husband or wife.

Saul said the leads he obtained this way were much better than those obtained by door-to-door canvassing. When he used telephone prospecting the homeowner was more likely to listen to the closer. And there's another obvious benefit: Telemarketing is a much more efficient use of a salesperson's time.

- This method was also used for stores and factories. In these cases, the initial calls were made between 10 A.M. and 3 P.M. Businesspeople could be seen during business hours and reconfirmation of appointment was unnecessary.

Saul used another technique to sell storm windows and doors. A telephone canvasser would solicit appointments. Saul would then send a mechanic to take all the measurements. The mechanic would leave a brochure, a brief history of the company, and a contract stating the number of windows or doors to be installed and the price.

The mechanic would have ten to twenty measuring jobs in a day. After returning to the office, the mechanic (who was also a salesperson) would call the homeowner at a pre-arranged time. If the family had an extension phone, the salesperson would make a presentation to both husband and wife. If there were no extension, the salesperson would find out who the decision-maker was and speak to that person. If the homeowner agreed to buy, all that was needed was a signature on the contract. Once the contract was mailed to the company, the work could begin.

If the deal could not be consummated over the phone, the salesperson would say:

> You know, it's difficult to do business over the phone. If I come to see you two, I know I can adjust this situation because I want to work with you.

This, of course, gave the salesperson another try and a better chance for success. Why better? Most likely the deal wasn't closed over the phone because the homeowner objected to something. The salesperson, knowing the objection, had time to think of a solution.

Cold Calling for Big Ticket Items

In the movie *Wall Street*, one scene depicts Bud Fox, a securities broker, being urged by his sales manager to cold call for prospects. Rather than face the redundancy of cold calling smaller investors for trading funds, Fox looks for the big fish. Gordon Gecko is the big-time inside trader whom Fox finally contacts, at first by telephone.

Aside from the entertainment value of such a movie, the script inadvertently touches on the real problem of the broker's fear of cold calling.

Cold calling for big ticket items requires patience and enthusiasm. The length of time that telemarketing for large orders takes must be extended for as long as the prospect remains fascinated. I said "fascinated," not interested. There is a difference. Big sales are complicated. Sales involving thousands of dollars hold a certain amount of fascination, as opposed to just interest, at the beginning of an explanation. The cold call therefore takes more time, more patience, and more expertise. Big money holds too much mystique to be passed over in three to five minutes.

The tone of your voice while giving the sales presentation must match the proposition. You must also explain the product thoroughly. The excitement in the cold caller's voice must complement the seriousness of the sale.

Benefits must be alluded to, but never given fully on the cold call. The history of the product is also vital. The cold caller, as always, must state the company's name, the company's state of origin, the protection that the prospect would have in the event of bankruptcy, the licensing, and the local representation.

If insurance is offered, final payouts to the insurance policyholders must be quoted precisely: The literature you mail should

have the premium schedule and other information to back up what
is said on the cold call.

Selling Financial Services

Investments require other considerations in the cold calling
effort. You must always stay within the rules and regulations of the
overseeing regulatory bodies and not violate those rules with your
enthusiasm. Exaggerated claims must be avoided in quoting returns
on investments and speculations.

If you can document a good past history for the product, it will
contribute to the fascination, and later, the interest, of the prospect.
The deeper interest the prospect has will surface after receiving and
reading your literature. The literature must be of the highest quality
paper and printing. It must be in good taste, with nothing ostenta-
tious, and the copy must be clearly written to avoid misrepresentation.

The financial services cold caller, with the very first words
uttered, must exhibit a certain voice firmness and discipline that
the sale or management of money requires. The cold caller's first
impressions can make or break a future close. When responding to
the prospect's fascination with money, the telephone salesperson
should treat the prospect's questions with extended answers while
seeking out the prospect's investment philosophy.

Questions pertaining to the size of the order, delivery, or
performance should be quoted in appropriate terms, leaving the
door open should there be an unexpected change in the financial
markets.

The prospect's philosophy need not be the same as that of the
broker-salesperson.

One young bond broker told me how he canvassed 133 calls
per day and had some possibilities for closing later on in future
telephone calls. When I pointed out that this was too many calls in
an eight-hour day and it reflected the fact that he was not spending
enough time searching out the philosophy of the people he was
calling, he changed his ways in the following weeks.

Now, in his extended conversations on first calls, he tries to uncover his prospects' investment strategies. If a prospect doesn't have an investment strategy, he takes the time to question the prospect about how much capital is available to invest and the return expectations. He then submits several plans to his prospects. What is he really doing? He is nurturing his prospect along, being empathetic and conscientious, and making a "buck" for himself in the altruistic environment that he created out of the prospect's initial fascination with money.

To summarize, financial services hold a certain amount of fascination for a prospect. This fascination must be turned into real interest on the first call. Therefore, the call should be extended to whatever time is needed to search out a matching philosophy.

If the prospect is busy call back on an appointment basis. Do not under any circumstances mail information without first determining the financial philosophy of the prospect. You could be wasting your time. Stock, insurance or commodity brokers have many products to sell—find the particular product suitable for your prospect.

Other than extending the time of the first call because of the powerful attitude that money provokes in a prospect, all cold calling follows the same rules as described in the cold calling chapter.

Let's Go to the Movies

With just a telephone, a pad and pencils, and the script for a film, a former stock and commodity broker with whom I worked for many years raised $2 million in one year to complete the production of a motion picture. Since he is such a good example of the success you can reap combining great selling skills and determination, the story of the process he went through will unfold as you continue reading. I shall call him "Richard the Moviemaker."

How did he do it? By cold calling from a list he purchased from a list company. The prospects' names and phone numbers cost him twelve cents each. They had the right financial profile with above average income, and need of a tax shelter because of their income level. Movies, in those days provided a tax shelter.

Richard the Moviemaker's opening lines were the same in every instance. They were honest and candid. They went like this:

"Mr. Johnson, this is Richard the Moviemaker calling." (Answer to the prospect's first question—I wonder who's calling? Why it's Richard the Moviemaker!) "I found your name through a list of investors and I want to propose an honest and interesting investment proposition to you for investing in an honest company." (Answer to the prospect's second question of why should I listen. Because he is an investor and there is the possibility of money to be made if he listens.)

Richard the Moviemaker pauses and changes the inflection of his voice from cordiality to the deep resonant tone that expresses money language.

Mr. Prospect, investors have made tremendous returns in movie productions either in sheltered or real income. Have you ever thought of participating in a movie production?" (This statement is the answer to the third question the prospect has in his mind, "What's in it for me?" There could be either one of two reasons, or both: the fascination of the return on investment or the lure of Hollywood celebrity status. Both were psychological factors in Richard's success in cold calling.)

Spending as much time on the first call as the prospect's *fascination* dictated, Richard alternately spoke and listened for the feedback from the prospect. In answering Richard's query, "Have you ever thought of participating in a movie production?" the prospects betrayed their feelings of fascination about the subject even though prospects always try to temper their interest when speaking to a salesperson for fear of being taken advantage of.

Fascination is always based on shallow information. It is the first step towards a deeper involvement.

Movies are pure fantasy in a sense. They help people escape from the boredom of everyday life.

The potential investors whose tendency was to fantasize the Hollywood life responded to Richard's question, "I have always wondered how movies were put together."

Richard: [*Sensing this fascination*] Mr. Prospect, you are familiar with how a building is constructed, I'm sure.

Prospect: Yes.

Richard: [*Continuing the metaphor*] There is nothing on the ground at the beginning, so you go to an engineer or an architect who draws up a set of plans. You then buy the construction materials and hire crews to supply the labor and, before you know it, the building is completed.

Prospect: Ah huh!

[*Richard continues without hesitation, because he knows he has stimulated the prospect's fascination into interest.*]

Richard: I have a plan, a 120-page plan including the budget for the film, the stars who are under contract to perform in it, and an artist's rendering of the set!

[*Now Richard waited for a reaction to his statement that just like the builder he had a plan. There was silence on the other end of the phone. The prospect had been frightened, for he expected the book to be offered to him. Now Richard has to take the risk of having his words rejected. He does this by prompting a further reaction.*]

Richard: If you have some serious interest, Mr. Prospect, I would like to send the prospectus to you for study. This is an investment that is not for everybody—only for a group of elite investors who are qualified in the sense that they can take some speculative risk, say for $100,000 or more.

The prospect has been qualified for the first time. The reaction that followed the last statement varied from prospect to prospect. Since the 120-page prospectus is costly to print, there must be prudent judgment in sending it only to those who responded positively. Prospects reply in various ways. For example:

"That's a little too rich for my blood, anything smaller?" Or, "Did anybody I know invest in it yet?" "That is not for me, I'm a little short of cash right now." "Send it along. I'd like to show it to my financial advisor." "What is the track record of the principals?" There were many different responses, some espousing interest in the proposition, others ruling it out completely.

Richard continued to qualify his prospects and found many seriously interested investors. Within one week he cold called 300 people, isolating 56 good prospects.

DOS AND DON'TS OF MAKING THE ULTIMATE CONNECTION

DO

Try always to telephone business prospects in off hours. Retail customers can be called at most anytime but holidays. If they are busy, make an appointment to call back at a specific time and keep the appointment.

DON'T

Deliberately mislead the prospect's secretary into thinking you are someone else or that you have urgent business. This kind of tactic always backfires.

DO

Call before or after normal business hours if you can't get past the secretary. You can only hope the prospect will pick up the phone.

DON'T

Be neurotically persistent. It is a waste of time and energy because you could be canvassing or selling someone else who is really interested in your product.

DO

Be understanding when young children answer the phone. Speak softly and always make it clear you will call back. Never leave a message with a young child other than to say "It is not important."

DON'T

Create systems for getting additional leads by unethical methods. If a premium is offered for an in-home appointment, make sure you bring it, especially if it is a no obligation offer. Doing business in an ethical manner perpetuates the company and your career. Do not participate in any lower business standards!

Chapter 5

SALES MEETING ON COLD CALL SELLING

Question: *What are the advantages of cold calling for leads over an advertised lead program? Cold calling seems time consuming. If leads were provided, a salesperson could be closing twice as many instead of looking for people to sell. Isn't an advertising program for prospects fairer to a commission salesperson? Wouldn't the telephone salesperson, as well as the house, make a lot more money?*

Answer: Let me answer your last question first. Advertising is expensive. A telephone salesperson cannot expect to make the same rate of commission if advertised leads are provided because of the high cost of media time and space.

For example, one company I know supplies prospects to salespeople from advertising. Payout is 8.5 percent commission on the gross sale on the opening of a new account and 5.5 percent on a reorder. A company in the same industry selling the same product pays 11.5 percent sales commission on everything, including reorders. The second company's main supply of customers is from cold calling. It provides lists to call from and will, on occasion, supply prospects to its salespeople from TV or direct mail advertising. This is a sensible approach.

Let me give you another example. A nationally known money market fund that advertises on network television gets 5,000 calls per advertisement on an incoming 800 number. These calls come to a central location. Information is mailed to each prospect. The company closes whatever it can by mail, but it has accumulated 250,000 names that never responded to the direct mailing. I was asked to set up a telemarketing group using these names as a starting point. I was also promised all the names that called in after future commercials who did not buy by mail. I showed these fund executives why the one-minute $350,000 commercial could not be profitable to them. The fund could just as well have used the phone book or street directory. Telemarketing using the television response names meant putting on 200 commission brokers. They might be paid a minimum of 2 percent commission, but the company would lose a great deal more money because of additional costs (telephone bills and postage). These costs made the company change its mind. They were better off paying by the hour to have clerks continue to send out materials.

But there are situations in mass TV, newspapers, or radio that directly or indirectly help in cold calling. These operations are highly commendable, but they are indirect. They supplement telemarketing. Take national companies like Merrill Lynch. They have institutionalized their company name by national advertising. When one of their brokers cold calls from a list of prospects, their company name is recognized and has an unconscious connotation of trust and reliability to the investor. One more important factor: A prospect, even though he may have faith in one company more than another, relies on the salesperson's charisma more than on whom the salesperson represents.

Advertising campaigns for high-priced items such as investments, construction, or real estate listings, only skim the surface of the marketplace. You don't dig into it unless you aggressively cold call. That is where the real marketplace for your product or service is hiding. Why? Because the marketplace underneath the advertising is bigger. It consists of passive people who do not act until they are prompted by someone calling them. This is a gold mine that we know is there. It is just a question of tapping into the vein!

Let me give you another example:

Just look what happened on Wall Street after the crash of October 19, 1987. The firms whose retail salespeople had always canvassed or cold called survived. Those who had depended on advertising for leads did not. The cold calling broker-salespeople are still making six-figure incomes. The advertisements of many firms who didn't train their people to cold call became more and more manipulative after the crash. Some even got themselves in trouble with the regulatory agencies. Most important of all, the public did not respond in mass to financial advertising because they were too frightened. But they did respond as individuals to other individuals whose voices over the phone gave advice and consolation. The investors felt these brokers demonstrated interest in their welfare by seeking them out.

Question: *Isn't cold calling really a game of numbers in the final analysis? If you call enough people you get enough positive responses to make the time spent worthwhile.*

Answer: I can't deny that, but take it a step further. If you just get on the phone and pound away at the push buttons without using any kind of technique, chances are you will get some prospects. But the quality of interest of those you do contact will be very poor.

You will get more and better prospects by putting in the same physical energy and adding some technique: Answer all the questions the prospect asks when the phone rings: "Do I want to be interrupted?" "I wonder who's calling?" "What's in it for me?" Introduce yourself in a tone of polite interruption, and chances are the prospects will find that your quick and smooth little speech will show them there is gain in a conversation with you. That is a good enough reason to listen.

You can call telephone soliciting a game of numbers, but it is how you react when talking to the people who comprise those numbers that determines the number who will agree to look at your literature and take a trial closing call from you.

If you want to take the approach of initially using your literature to sell your product or service, that is okay too. If the literature is good, and by that I mean well written, high quality paper, and appealing display, then you could have a good quality prospect also. The logic in putting the emphasis on the literature in the canvas call is that on the second call you can pick up the prospect's interest that was stimulated by your voice and now is aided by something tangible.

Question: *How long should a cold call last? One minute? Two or three or ten? You talk about using a three-minute egg timer to time the first call. Is that enough time to get your pitch across?*

Answer: That depends on the individual making the call, the speed of the delivery, the length of the words, and, of course, the prospect's answers. My suggestion of using an egg timer was to limit the information the cold caller gives about the product, to avoid going into a full presentation. It was intended to show that on a first call the emphasis should be on the proposition being sold and on the literature. The purpose of cold calling is to entice the prospect into listening to the whole story.

Question: *Suppose your prospect wants the whole story then and there? Do you give it?*

Answer: That, my friend, depends on the product or service for sale. For example, if you are a fund-raiser looking for $5 or $10, go ahead and ask for the donation on the first call. But even there, unless you have credentials that the prospect will recognize instantly, you'll have a hard time getting even that small amount of money.

The simple truth is when you attempt to sell capital goods or services for serious amounts of money, you should not do it in one call. It takes work and technique, including a serious explanation to the prospect. Otherwise it is unfair. I am not saying that it has not been done. In all probability, it is being done all over the country right now. Thousands of dollars might be changing hands on the strength of one phone call.

When parties to a transaction know each other, know what they are getting, and have dealt with each other before, there is nothing unusual about doing business on one call. Recommendations are also first call closes in some cases, but for a stock commodity or insurance broker or other person in a capital goods industry, a one call close is not likely.

This is one of the disadvantages of telephone sales. In field sales you can make a one call close. Papers and contracts and verifications all can be signed in the prospect's home or office. Money, in the form of deposits in check, cash, or credit card, can be transferred on the spot. So you can see, a telephone sale is a lot harder to close than a field sale. However, the other advantages of telephone selling over field selling are numerous. In my opinion, telephone sales are much more lucrative for the salesperson in the long run.

Question: *What do you mean when you say telephone cold calling or canvassing is a sifting process?*

Answer: Good question. Look at a cold calling effort from this
                   perspective: Every refusal to listen to your story brings
                   you that much closer to someone who will listen. In
                   effect, you are eliminating those who are not inter-
                   ested. It takes time but look at what you are accom-
                   plishing.

Question: *Your comments on cold calling phobia aren't clear to
                   me. Aren't telephone salespeople afraid of rejection?
                   Isn't that the real fear and the phobia?*

Answer: In all fairness to your question, I include rejection as
                   part of cold calling phobia. But that is at the lowest part
                   of the abstraction process of delving into human feel-
                   ing. Let me expand.

                   Everybody wants to be taken care of, prospects and
                   telephone salespeople alike. The subliminal effect most
                   advertising creates is to buy the product because it will
                   take care of you. It will add to your beauty, personality,
                   or life in general. In the same vein, salespeople prefer
                   advertised leads to cold calling because they feel they
                   are easier, and that the house, the company, or the
                   manager, by supplying advertised leads, are taking care
                   of them. But remember, the prospect is going to re-
                   spond because the advertisement said it was going to
                   take care of him.

                   In cold calling phobia, the salesperson does not
                   have self-confidence and needs management, not for
                   guidance and training, but for prospects who will be
                   sure buyers. These types of salespeople are emotionally
                   dependent because they think they are powerless. They
                   have a very limited psychological capacity and many of
                   them turn out to be unethical manipulators. You see,
                   lack of confidence and unethical manipulation are two
                   sides of the same coin.

                   Let us look at the reasons a salesperson develops
                   cold calling phobia. Some of you may remember the
                   emotional pain you felt when you began to cold call
                   and you were rejected. One thing I want you to
                   understand is that these fears did not develop when you

came into telephone sales. You had them before. For some of you, that was the reason you came to telephone sales; you felt you could repress your fears better if you were not seen. You transferred negative feelings about other people into telemarketing, but rationalization gave them a different meaning. In other words, you gave the original doubts about yourself a different form.

Think about the person who is a hundred pounds overweight and is ashamed of the way he looks. He uses telephone selling to hide his appearance. He'll do well because he realizes that people are not aware of how he looks. But sooner or later the feelings of worthlessness will recur and overpower the new reality.

Think about the black man who has been taught since infancy by the white community that he is not equal. If he can put aside his anger at a racist community, he'll do well. But if he cannot adjust to what is inside him, and if he feels he is hiding behind a telephone instead of working as an equal, the inner pressures will break through in his voice and his attitude.

Think about the person who has studied for a career, but because of economic or personal reasons can't pursue that career. Such men and women come into telephone selling grossly overqualified. They take telemarketing jobs as a means of economic survival. They don't have positive feelings about themselves because they think they have failed.

These kind of personal problems and feelings can hide behind a telephone for a while, but eventually they will reappear as if from nowhere. The person who cannot separate cold calling activities from personal life and feelings falls victim to the nature of the business: the hangups, the "not interested" answers, the anxiety, the impatience. Cold calling amplifies the terrible hurts the person has had in the past. Cold calling is too much to bear.

My advice is this: You overcome negative feelings
by stroking yourself. Be a better manager to yourself
than the one you have.

Question: *I have read all the positive things you have to say about
canvassing on the telephone, but I can't agree. I get so
many disconnected telephones, people who have died,
people who have moved on. Since I do sell investments,
sometimes I spend ten to fifteen minutes with a prospect
because of the fascination aspect, but I don't think it
pays. Without cold calling my phone bill could be cut
down considerably and my time would be saved for
better things. What you call the sorting process gets me
down. After a while, it gets disgusting and I feel burnt
out.*

Answer: Let me suggest something to you—but first, I want to
ask, what kind of financial instruments do you sell?

Question: *Commodities.*

Answer: That is an easy one! What time does the last market
close?

Question: *Depends on what market I am in. The last two close at
3:00 P.M. and 4:00 P.M.*

Answer: What hours are you cold calling now?

Question: *All day long, intermittently.*

Answer: It is obvious why you feel burnt out. I would suggest to
you that while you are trading you refrain from cold
calling. Save that for after the close of market, and set
aside at least three nights a week and some Saturday
afternoons. Also, Sunday evening at about 6:00 P.M. is
a good time for cold calling.

Question: *Wouldn't that disturb people and alienate them?*

Answer: It would disturb some, but not those who would have
some interest—and those are the people you are seeking. Look at it this way: On Sunday night in the United
States it is Monday in the Far East and they are trading
the dollar already.

Stock brokers and some insurance people can also
use Sunday evening profitably. Most investments hang
on how the U.S. dollar's value is holding up. People

selling capital goods cannot do this because the buyers they want are not available at this time.

As far as disconnects and dead people, that is a very real problem. Too many of those can burn out even the best salespeople. Show the manager your call sheet. You can tell by the dispositions how good your calling list is and then act accordingly.

Question: *Your appraisal of what goes through the prospect's mind when the phone rings confuses me. I can see a prospect saying to herself, "I wonder who is calling?" I do that myself. But as far as, "Why should I listen or what is in it for me?" I don't think I have ever asked myself those questions. When I get a solicitation call, I just cut it off. I tell them, "No thanks," and hang up.*

Answer: You really think so? Well, let me prove to you that you do. But you must understand first that all human beings want some *sensation* as part of their self-gratification process in living. The definition of sensation is a mental or physical stimulation brought on in this case (telephone selling) by another person's voice. That is what is in it for you! For example, are you married?

Question: *No, I'm not.*

Answer: Got a fiancée or a steady girlfriend?

Question: *Yes, I do.*

Answer: When was the last time you saw her?

Question: *Two nights ago.*

Answer: Have you spoken to her on the phone since then?

Question: *No, I haven't, but she will call me tonight or I will call her.*

Answer: That is exactly my point! You are looking forward to that call, aren't you?

Question: *Yes, I am!*

Answer: And you are going to listen to her when she calls because there is something in it for you—a sensation! I have used this highly personal situation to prove a point. If the voice of a solicitor is pleasant, there is a sensation for the recipient of that call, and that is reason enough to listen. As far as "What's in it for me?" that is going to depend on what the product is. Does the prospect have any need or want for it? The reason you hang up so abruptly and say, "No, thank you," probably has to do with your finances. Am I correct in assuming that you are trying to save all the money you can and are not buying anything and feel vulnerable to salespeople?

Question: *How did you know?*

Answer: Because fear is a sensation also. When you put your hand on something hot, you pull it away immediately before you get hurt. That is why a lot of people hang up. I refer to it as fight or flight. Fear puts a damper on positive sensation.

Part Three

TRIAL CLOSING

Chapter 6

THE SECOND SALES CALL IS THE TRIAL CLOSE

The purpose of the cold call is to find good prospects—people whose buying interest you think you can develop. Each prospect is then sent printed information about your product or service and your company. These materials will help you accomplish the purpose of the second call—the trial close—to turn these prospects into customers.

What to Avoid

You must avoid certain words and topics at this stage. As in the beginning of any relationship, both prospect and salesperson are still unknown to each other. While these subjects may well come up in a later conversation, when both parties are comfortable with each other, they should be avoided at this time.

- Name dropping
- Vulgarity
- Uncommon words
- Clichés
- Old stories
- Politics and religion
- Personal observations
- Stories about your children
- Digressions from the subject matter of your product or service
- Any attempt to pry into a prospect's personal life. Accept personal information only if the prospect volunteers it
- Gossip about other people

Most telephone salespeople are more concerned with the number of calls they make than the quality of those calls. Concern yourself with quality. And be sure your calls show courtesy and consideration for your prospect. The time you take for courtesy will pay off.

What If the Prospect Is Just "Not Interested"?

Some prospects won't want to hear your sales presentation, even though they were somewhat positive during the original cold call. They will say, at the beginning of the second call, "I've looked your material over and I'm not interested."

You've already made an investment in this prospect. What do you do now? Do you continue to spend your time on this prospect or do you cut your losses? Is there a possibility you can sell to this prospect? And how can you find this out now?

When the prospect says, "I'm not interested," he's intimating that he's read your material and evaluated its contents. Most salespeople will, in the name of a positive attitude, try to directly repudiate the prospect's evaluation of the sales literature:

You're wrong, Mr. Prospect. This is the carpet sweeper of the eighties. Your store should be selling it.

The prospect's answer may be:

Well, I don't think so, Mr. Salesperson. I'm satisfied with the one I now sell. I don't need a new brand.

Vanity comes to surface when you tell a prospect that his evaluation process is inadequate. Most people don't like to be told they don't know their own business.

But that doesn't mean you should give up the investment you've already made in your prospect. You owe it to yourself to test the prospect's personality. While some people will reject you and your product, or even hang up, if you hint at their inability to evaluate, others are comfortable with evaluations being made for them; they don't get upset when their judgment is criticized.

You can test the prospect's personality with an inquiry:

Salesperson: Mr. Prospect, is this a personal decision not to buy, or do you see some deficiency in the sweeper as compared to the competition? Engineers are great when they design something like this, but I'd really like to know what a person with your practical experience sees. Possibly you could help me by pointing out a deficiency.

[Now that the ball is in the prospect's court, the response may be as follows.]

Prospect: No, no. There's nothing wrong in the manufacture, it's just that I'm satisfied with the one we're selling now.

[It's plain that the prospect hasn't evaluated the item mechanically at all. He's just comfortable with the product he's now selling. If this is the response you get, you may say something like the following.]

Salesperson: Oh, I see. What brand are you selling in your store?
Prospect: "Easy Sweeper."

Salesperson: Oh, I've heard of the Easy Sweeper, Mr. Prospect, and I
                   have to point out a feature that my machine has that it
                   doesn't have.

You can then move smoothly into your presentation.

If, on the other hand, the prospect responds to your initial
question by telling you about a specific feature that Easy Sweeper
has and your product lacks, criticizing will only cement your
failure. But even in this case you may be successful if your product
has a feature the competition doesn't have. Highlight that feature
and see if it's important to your prospect.

There's also another possibility. Some prospects continually
dangle the possibility of a sale, leading you to chase a promise that
will never be fulfilled. Telemarketers call people who do this
"strokers." These people are using you for their own neurotic
reasons. Use your knowledge of human nature and your ability to
"read" your prospects to protect yourself from wasting time with
"strokers."

Establishing Credibility

The business relationship you have with the sales prospect requires
that you provide some information about yourself. The prospect
wants to know who you are, what company you work for, and
something about your company before making a decision to buy.
This kind of information helps establish your credibility and reliability.

"Lecturing" the Prospect

After you've given the prospect some information about yourself,
you must give some information about the product or service you're
selling. This is what your "lecture" is all about. It's probably the
most important part of the sales process.

As you may remember from listening to lectures in school,
words are fleeting. The listener's concentration level is not always

high. The prospect may not be listening to you as intently as you would hope.

You must help the prospect concentrate on what you're saying. The printed information which the prospect has received can help. If the prospect has it at hand it will serve as a backup to your spoken words, both during your presentation and afterward. One way to use this literature is to refer directly to it during your lecture, just as a teacher might refer to written handouts. Refer to specific sentences, paragraphs, or graphic material. Or, ask the prospect to follow along as your comments parallel the written information.

Another way to make sure the prospect is concentrating on what you're telling her is to ask her to write down specific facts. You can say, "Ms. Prospect, do you have a pencil and paper handy? I'd like you to jot down some important fact about this product." Writing the information down will often make it stick in the prospect's mind.

Your challenge is to convince prospects that what you're selling has unique value, either to them personally or to their business. You must show that your product or service will enhance the prospects' life or business—that its value *to them* is worth its cost.

The successful telephone sales conversation is a personalized conversation. People desperately want personalized attention. Discount stores, computers, and many other aspects of the current business world have eliminated personalized selling, but it still exists in telephone sales. That's why telephone sales rooms are opening up all around the country. People want to be treated as special when they spend their money. The telephone salesperson is in direct contact with the prospect and can search out the uniqueness of the prospect's needs or wants. With this information, the effective salesperson can then persuade the prospect that the product or service fits those specifications. Talking computers and large display ads can't do this.

The prime subject matter of the sales conversation should be the product or service to be sold. The conversation should run on two parallel levels. On one level, you use words to describe what you're selling. On the other level, you should develop the prospect's interest with a rich and resonant tone of voice. These two levels should complement each other. Your words must fit your tone of voice or you'll sound choppy instead of confident. Your words should focus on the research that developed your product or service and documented observations about its performance.

Use step-by-step logic again and again to substantiate your contention that the product fits the prospect's needs. This will lead you into the next stage of the sales call—the testimonial.

The Testimonial

Now you urge the prospect into action (placing an order) by giving a testimonial for the product or service. At this point in the conversation your partiality should be very obvious. Praise yourself, your company, and your product. Use a strong voice and language that suits your personality.

Don't moderate your passion for what you're selling. Prospects are reassured by a salesperson with a strong belief in the product.

Answer all of your prospect's questions. The answers will help form a connection between you and the prospect, and this connection is vital if the sale is to be closed successfully.

You can gain favor with your prospect by pointing out a small meaningless defect in your product or service. This shows your honesty, especially if the prospect knows or thinks you're working on a straight commission. This isn't a new sales practice, but it is effective. Just think of Avis' "We're Number Two, but we try harder" campaign.

Using Inferences

An inference is a statement of logical conclusion. It is to some degree probable but not verifiable.

If you say of competitor ABC that it "sold off its real estate holdings quite suddenly when its hair dryer line didn't sell," the inference is that ABC is in financial trouble.

If you say "my company is probably the largest manufacturer of hair dryers in the world since we bought ABC's hair dryer line," the inference is that your company is the best hair dryer manufacturer in the world.

Inferences can be an effective part of your sales presentation. They can slant the prospect's thinking—postively toward you and your company and negatively toward your competitor—without direct negative comments or boasts. And if you let the prospect make the inference it can be more effective than a direct statement because the prospect is participating in the process.

Examine these two statements. Neither is entirely verifiable; both are slanted, but they can help persuade someone to buy from you. Remember, a sales presentation isn't a report. It's a biased, opinionated conversation slanted toward persuading the prospect to buy from you instead of the competition.

Some "reporting" does take place. Your statement about ABC's sale of its real estate holdings is a statement of fact. So is your statement about your company's purchase of ABC's hair dryer line. Both are verifiable, but the inferences that arise from these statements, that ABC is in financial trouble and that your company is the world's best hair dryer manufacturer, are not so easily verified.

Use discretion in creating an inference. If you go beyond the factual statements and draw the inference yourself, say "in my opinion." This clearly indicates that the inference could be mistaken:

> In my opinion, Ms. Prospect, ABC is having some financial difficulty because of the failure of its hair dryer line. With its line, we're now probably one of the largest and best in the world.

Use inferences to allow the prospect to draw positive conclusions about the value and benefits of you and your product and negative conclusions about your competitor. Then move to bring the sales presentation to its close.

The Trial Close

You've made your case for your product or service. Now you must ask for the order. Asking for the order on the second call is known as a trial close. It's your first attempt to get the order. You could say:

Ms. Prospect, I know your industry and I know how perfect my product fits into the needs of your business and how helpful it could be. Will you please give me your okay to ship?

More than likely, the answer will be, "Well, I want to think about it," or a similar evasive response. You thought your presentation was perfect and your heart sinks at such an answer. But don't despair. You had to get the first closing attempt out of the way. In responding to it the prospect reveals the first line of sales resistance. It's up to the good salesperson to overcome that resistance and any resistance that follows.

Sales Resistance—And What to Do About It

Sales resistance is a natural response, as natural as pulling one's fingers away from a hot stove. The prospect is asking himself, "Do I need this product?" and "Is it worth the cost?"

If a sales presentation is good it puts opposing forces to work within your prospect. Whether or not the prospect will be willing to buy depends upon the facts that are predominant in his mind. The forces that oppose the buy challenge everything you say, but the prospect may not verbalize these forces. It's important, therefore, not to become too overbearing. Keep the prospect at ease and be sure written material is on hand for the prospect's easy reference. That material can reaffirm all or part of your presentation.

A good sales presentation is, in effect, an attack on the status quo because it is asking for a change—a change that costs money. This is so regardless of whether what you're trying to sell is something the prospect needs or something that will enhance his life.

Money is the underlying serpent whose rigidity and influence may dictate the course of the sale. It's not the immediate focus of the sale—the product or service is—but except for impulse buyers it is a concern for most people. Sales resistance thus can come as a result of a limited budget.

Sales resistance may also be caused by the prospect's fear of making an error in judgment. The prospect looks to you for guidance in making a final decision. If you don't know or understand the product or service you're selling, the prospect will immediately sense that and will be unwilling to use your help in making the buying decision. Similarly, if you don't respond adequately to the prospect's questions, stated or not, about the product, the prospect won't be willing to rely on you in making the buying decision and will not place the order.

Many salespeople make a major effort when they first face the prospect's resistance. They respond with excessive anxiety. Afraid of possible failure, they try to cover up their fear by using sales hype. They build themselves up with emotionalism and then project this emotionalism onto the prospect. The anxious salesperson creates an invalid sense of urgency.

Sales hype is seen as a quick, easy way to break the prospect's sales resistance, but it seldom works. This kind of sales approach is ineffective and borders on fraud and misrepresentation. You may make a few sales this way, but you won't get repeat business.

What then should you do to fight your prospect's sales resistance? You must use persuasion instead of hype. Listen carefully to your prospect's questions or comments. Answer the questions and deal with the comments as they arise. Your objective is to persuade your prospect of the benefits of your product and that it's worth the cost.

Clear and concise explanations and answers are the best way to penetrate any prospect's defenses. It is also the best way to get the prospect to make an affirmative buying decision. And if you succeed this way, rather than with sales hype, your prospect is more likely to turn into a repeat customer.

Sales resistance will pop up again and again as the prospect interrupts your presentation with questions and comments. Don't get annoyed at these interruptions. Instead use them to further your sales talk. The prospect is trying to get the facts—facts about the product's usefulness, its construction, its price and warranties. Show the prospect the benefits of buying the product. Highlight the product's value *to this particular prospect* and prove it's "worth the price."

Try to answer all questions and respond to all negative comments. A question that goes unanswered or a negative comment left unrebutted can destroy your entire sales presentation. It can break the continuity of your sales talk and lose you the sale.

In answering the prospect's questions, be careful not to negate the forward movement of your sales presentation. Answer each question, but don't stop there. Use the questions to help you judge the prospect's perceptions, fears, and concerns. Try to understand the prospect's underlying thoughts. Phrase your answers so that the prospect will identify with you. It's this connection between you and the prospect that makes the sale.

Remember, prospects will never expose needs and wants completely, because they don't really understand what they are. But once you've established a connection, prospects will in effect give you permission to delve further. You'll be able to ask enough so you can learn the prospects needs. And if you're knowledgeable about the product or service you're selling, you can then point out benefits as they directly apply to them. You'll be successful in making the sale because of your patience and your knowledge—knowledge of your product and knowledge of human nature.

Finally, in dealing with your prospects' questions, don't allow yourself to get caught up in a rhythm of question, answer, question, answer.

If a prospect is strangely silent early in the presentation, probe to discover the real reason for the sales resistance so you can confront it. Sales resistance can be hard to pin down if the prospect doesn't verbalize it.

Chapter 7

MANIPULATION

There are other techniques that can help you overcome your prospect's sales resistance. They are all based on one thing: influencing the prospect by manipulation.

Manipulation, because it is used in everyday life, must be put into proper perspective.

When I first mentioned using the word "manipulative" and describing its use in selling, my colleagues were horrified. One even went so far as to advise me that the federal regulatory body that governs the industry I am working in would take a dim view of my referring to a manipulative technique. My answer is that the people who deny their own manipulative efforts are not facing reality.

Manipulating our environment is how we earn our living. Manipulation comes quite naturally to all humans early in life. By the age of two we are all experts. Manipulation and survival go together at that early age. The infant learns that cries in the night bring Mommy or Daddy. The baby learning to talk finds that saying

"Mama" brings a smile. The toddler learns that touching some household objects brings a reprimand.

We learn, as small children, that our actions can cause the people around us to react in certain ways. We use that knowledge of human behavior to manipulate. As children, our goal may be another cookie or a later bedtime.

The psychology textbooks say that parents should instill confidence by substituting self-power for manipulation. In this way the child achieves mastery over its own life. But a small amount of manipulation stays with us.

One can resort to a manipulative effort to gain a prospect's attention in cold calling and at the beginning of the follow-up call, if need be, but knowledge of one's product and some knowledge of human behavior is what closes the deal. Manipulation has no real depth to it. Its effects on others are not lasting. We call people who only use manipulation phonies.

When manipulation is used unethically, the salesperson encourages the prospect to buy something not needed or pay more than a product is worth. The prospect does it to maintain certain important beliefs. To give you an example, the prospect may be satisfied because by paying more than something's worth, or by buying something not needed, it reinforces the "always a victim, but I can overcome the vicissitudes of life on the road to perfection" rule. Or by buying unneeded things, the act of spending money gives a sense of power.

These reasons to buy may sound preposterous to you, but many people have hidden agendas that cause them to buy for just such reasons. They may not even be aware of the games they're playing because their denial processes are so strong.

The salesperson often has a hidden agenda too. When a salesperson is successful in unethical manipulation by charging a higher-than-usual price, or by selling something the prospect doesn't need, or misrepresenting a product's performance, often the motive is not money. The sale is a way for the salesperson to prove "I am smarter than everyone else and am, therefore, on my way to perfection." That is what's important to that salesperson.

The reality of life is simple. There isn't any perfection in human beings. A sale cannot be *successfully* closed by unethical manipulation. If you get an order by unethically manipulating the prospect, rather than through an exchange of ideas about a product or service with value, the quality of that order must be seriously questioned. Will you get paid? And if you do get paid, will you get a repeat order? When the prospect is unethically manipulated—or, to be blunt, used—often the salesperson, as well as the buyer, must beware.

We shall explore manipulation further in closing sales and demystify those salespeople and businesspeople who set themselves apart as perfect sales models.

For a sale to be successful, two elements are necessary. First, the salesperson must emphasize quality, performance, and price. Then the benefits the prospect will receive must be explained. There must never be any doubt about what the salesperson will provide in terms of service and value.

Second, the salesperson must expose and then examine the prospect's hidden agenda, if there is one, and must find out the prospect's expectations about the produce or service. If the prospect expects more than the product or service can provide, the salesperson must either clarify what is available from the company and, if necessary, from a competitor, or in some way moderate the prospect's expectations.

It's only when these two elements are present that goodwill can result. And if there is goodwill, a commercial bond between salesperson and prospect can be cemented.

Imagine, if you will, a stockbroker, on a second call to a prospect:

Stockbroker: Ms. Prospect, my philosophy has always been to protect a client's equity as best I can and to stay within speculative limits for people over age fifty. Are you in that age category?

Prospect: I'm sixty-five, but I've got plenty of money and I don't mind speculating with $10,000–20,000.

The stockbroker has exposed the prospect's hidden agenda: She wants to speculate and can afford to do so. If the stockbroker had instead asked, "How old are you?" without telling of his own philosophy of investing for people over fifty, it's likely the prospect would not have revealed her own beliefs. The salesperson revealed his own philosophy and that prompted the prospect to do the same.

But the prospect's response to the stockbroker's question might be a negative one. The prospect might reply, "Never you mind, you just tell me what you've got that I could make money with."

Hearing this kind of response, the salesperson must ask himself why the prospect has such an attitude. She may have had losses in the past, or bad experiences with other salespeople, or she might think that her chances for success, for getting an edge, are better if she hides her personal agenda. After all, it's true in poker that you're more likely to win if you keep your cards to yourself. If this is the prospect's attitude, the salesperson must let the prospect know that selling isn't a game. The salesman needs all the necessary details in order to be effective:

> Ms. Prospect, your attitude leads me to believe that you fear I will take advantage of you. Quite the contrary! I won't harm you in any way. Investments are a cooperative effort. Hopefully both of us gain. I get my selling price for the company, which includes my salary, and you get good present value.
>
> Unless I know what your philosophy is, I can't personalize a program for you. My purpose is to have an ongoing customer-company relationship where we both are successful.

I never use unethical manipulation, and I never knowingly tolerate such methods from the people who work for me.

But there are certain tools of ethical manipulation you can use to penetrate sales resistance. They are:

1. Mutual admiration between salesperson and prospect—showing you care
2. Doing favors
3. Limiting the time of the offer
4. Celebrity and expert endorsements
5. Other tools of ethical manipulation

We shall examine each of these tools so you can see how and why they work to penetrate your prospect's sales resistance. Many telephone salespeople intuitively use these techniques without an understanding of why they work. These techniques can be even more successful if you know why they work so well.

The techniques described below exploit personality traits common to most people. But remember, for a sale to be successful, each party must benefit. You receive a commission or salary. The prospect must receive something of value too: your product or service.

Goodwill Between Salesperson and Prospect: Showing You Care

People like doing business with someone who is friendly and pleasant. This sales approach has consistently helped me. I like most people and they like me, and it makes my sales job easier. Prospects who trust your judgment are more likely to give you their order.

I treat my customers as important people. Their needs and interests take precedence in our relationship. I make an effort to learn about each customer's business and personal life, how the business or job is going, the important personal problems, how much she can afford to spend, her needs, and so on. I use this information to make the customers feel comfortable about doing business with me. In our conversations I verbalize the positive aspects of how I feel about them.

When you learn about your customers, you can identify with them, creating a "good guy" situation. This allows you to call them back, even after a rejection. Knowing their needs and staying objective about them works in the long run, even though it means you lose a few sales here and there.

Put energy into the interaction between you and your prospects. Show them you care. You'll find you can openly ingratiate yourself with prospects even though they're aware that you're doing it for business reasons. One way to do this is to send greeting cards. Joe Girard, a car salesman, developed a great manipulative technique. He sent each of his customers a card with the words, "I like you," on the card. It was sincere and it worked. The card helped him form a bond with his customers. This bond, along with his expertise and fair prices, allowed him to win the "Number One Car Salesman" award for eleven years in a row.

Remember, in sales your business is really people, not products or services. You can find something to like in everybody.

Doing Favors

When someone is especially nice, most people want to do something nice in return. When someone does you a favor, you want to do a favor in return. This is so in our personal dealings; it's also true in business. Many people feel obligated by a free gift or sample or trial offer. They feel they must return the favor by buying the product the next time. The Amway company has used this technique successfully for years.

If you don't have samples to send or free offers to present, the next best thing is to do your prospects a favor. Keep them informed of what's going on in the industry or profession. Scan the newspapers or trade magazines for items of interest to them. Send them your latest updated brochure with your business card every time you talk with them. You are providing a service and the prospects will feel obligated by it. You're also giving the prospects new information that you will be able to use, when the time comes, to close the sale.

Don't forget about your current customers. This technique works well with them also. It can help you build a solid relationship with your customers.

Doing favors—at least certain kinds of favors—works for another reason as well. If you can get people to try your product or service for a short time period, say, with a special promotion, they will probably turn into regular buyers if your product or service is of the expected quality. This works because most people generally prefer to avoid change. They like consistency in most aspects of their lives.

This personality trait affects salespeople in another important way. If a customer expresses extreme reaction to change don't focus on even the most positive changes in your product or service. Describe the product or service instead as slightly improved. Saying more will not help your sale. Let the buyer infer that the rewards of owning the product are slight. If the benefits are too large the prospect will worry about the risks involved or will think the benefits are too good to be true.

Limiting the Time of the Offer

Most people don't like to think they might miss something important. That's why they interrupt whatever they're doing to answer the phone, they go out of their way to go to a sale that's advertised as having limited supplies of specially priced goods, and they rearrange their plans to get to "special one-day" sales.

You can use this personality trait to help overcome your prospects' sales resistance. When you tell prospects that a special offer is a limited one, you are influencing their judgment by giving them a restrictive choice. You're giving them a directive to buy, and buy *now*. But be careful. If you push it too hard, the prospects will start thinking more carefully about your offer and will worry about being tricked. This technique will work only if you present it with a "take it or leave it" attitude.

I frequently use this technique and I find it to be effective. If it doesn't work right away, I don't press the issue. I always end my presentation with these words: "Well, just as the sun will come up tomorrow, there's always another deal, so I'll get you the next time."

With that comment I sometimes get an immediate change of attitude from the prospect. He wants to buy my product. And if the comment doesn't cause a change in the prospect's mind, I've laid groundwork for the next sale. In either event, the prospect remains a good one.

Celebrity and Expert Endorsements

Endorsements work because people associate celebrities and experts, on a deep psychological level, with their parents. An expert's endorsement is seen as a parental directive like the frequently remembered one to "Eat this; it's good for you." Celebrity endorsements work because the prospect associates the celebrity with the company. If the prospect has good feelings about the celebrity, the prospect will have good feelings about the company as well.

The endorsement of either an expert or a celebrity will help you overcome the prospect's uncertainty over whether or not to make the purchase. It can be a very effective tool.

As a telephone salesperson you can use endorsements even if your company's advertising doesn't. References—names of those who have used your product or service—can serve as indirect endorsements. Don't use individuals you've sold to as references. Use their businesses. And be sure to ask for permission first.

You can even use successful but unknown people, without using their names:

> Mr. Jones, I can only say that XYZ product is used by a certain well-known individual in the area.
> Now, this person is very discriminating in his purchases and use of XYZ. His professional position doesn't allow him to make an outright endorsement. He's a very private person, so I can't use his name. I can only tell you he is a highly successful professional and he wouldn't be happy unless he had a good supply of XYZ in his home.

The prospect will make an inference about who the unnamed person is and that's exactly what you want to happen.

One mistake in using references is the failure to properly analyze your prospect. Let's say a temporary employment agency calls on the owner of a small business to solicit its business:

> This is the Happy Temporary Secretary Agency. We have serviced Citibank, IBM, and Chase Manhattan with temporary help. We'd like you to consider our services when you need a temp.

It's flattering to a small-businessperson to hear that a service that wants her business also works for such large companies, but such references, impressive as they are, will more likely hurt than help the agency get her business. She will probably assume that in an emergency her needs will be pushed aside in favor of the larger customer. She is likely to look elsewhere for help.

Analyze your prospect carefully before you use references as indirect endorsements. That way the references won't backfire on you.

Other Tools of Ethical Manipulation

There are many other tools of ethical manipulation. They aren't logical because they arise from idiosyncrasies in people's personalities. But they work. You'll learn about these other tools as you speak to your prospects.

Two examples: Some people believe the more money they spend the better the product or service will be. They want to spend more than their neighbor. Other people, even though they have a small amount to spend, want to hear about the more expensive item. You can close the sale with these prospects by telling them, "I have a less expensive item that's just as good."

Americans are immature buyers. They don't investigate or think things through. They leave major decisions to others, including salespeople, so that if something goes wrong they won't have to be responsible. You can use these personality traits—in other words, manipulate your prospects—to sell your product or service, but be careful not to cross over the line to unethical manipulation. Be careful to keep your sales practices within the framework of good conscience and the law.

USING THE TOOLS OF ETHICAL MANIPULATION

Your use of the tools of ethical manipulation will vary from prospect to prospect. For one prospect, one or two may help you close on the second call; for another prospect, a different approach and half a dozen calls may be necessary.

In making these calls you must try to establish a connection with your prospect. That is, in fact, the whole purpose of the manipulative effort: to make an empathetic connection with the prospect. Once this is accomplished, your suggestion of what to buy and your discussion of the product's benefits will stimulate the close of the sale.

Disguised Sales Resistance

Sales resistance may be disguised. Rather than talk about problems or questions about the product, the prospect may raise other issues. You must train yourself to recognize sales resistance in its many forms. Some of the types of resistance salespeople run into most frequently include:

- Random conversation unrelated to the sales presentation
- Verbalizing personal problems—"I'm worried about my son who's with a babysitter today. You'll have to pardon my inattention"
- The prospect with limited time to talk
- Saying that the spouse is complaining about costs, or that the spouse (or the prospect) isn't working right now, and therefore the product or service can't be afforded at this time

When your prospect's response is "I have to ask my spouse" or "I don't have the money right now," it frequently reveals indecision or a lack of candor. Don't answer in a manipulative way. If the prospect indicates a need to consult with someone—a spouse or anyone else—indicate that you understand, and you'll call again, but go on to say you'd like the opportunity to be present or at least consulted at such a meeting. You might suggest a conference telephone call at your expense. That way you can deal with any questions that might arise. Questions left unanswered might cause you to lose the sale. A sincere prospect won't refuse your suggestion.

Your training manual may provide you with rebuttals for these types of comments, but these stereotyped answers usually don't work. They don't allow you to creatively personalize your sales presentation and therefore advance your sales talk toward a successful close. Avoid these "canned" responses. Respond to your prospect's resistance individually. You'll be much more successful that way.

And remember that the prospect is listening not only to the facts you present, he is also listening to, and being influenced by, the sound of your voice. If you sound sincere and confident the prospect will feel more confident about what you're selling.

You must deal with sales resistance. It won't just go away. You must actively seek it out and confront it to successfully overcome it. Your underlying message throughout your presentation should be your promise of customer satisfaction, and you must provide the facts backing up that promise. That message will overcome resistance.

Your enemy is the sales resistance, not the prospect. If, however, after all your efforts you find that the prospect's sales resistance is not realistic and manipulation doesn't help, you might as well move on to the next prospect. Nothing will help you close that sale.

A Note About "Control" of the Prospect

When I started out in sales I was advised to get "control" of the prospect. This control, as described, seemed much like the control you have over a car you are driving. Once I had control, I was told, the risk of rejection was small. I would get the sale.

I strived for this control for many years without ever fully understanding what it was. When I felt in control of a sales situation I saw that the prospect picked up on my suggestions, followed my advice in the purchases, and depended upon me. Was this the control I was told about during sales training? Or was it the trust and faith that comes from proving yourself to a prospect?

I have learned that a salesperson is in control of a prospect only by virtue of the prospect's *gift* to him of authority. That authority can be taken away as quickly as it was given. So control doesn't really exist. Influence over another person does.

In seeking this influence some salespeople use unethical manipulation. They attack the prospect's feelings with loaded words, fast talk, and emotionalism; they completely disregard the prospect's needs, and try to make the prospect entirely dependent on them for the buying decision.

Many a sales rep has come to me and said, "Bill Jones is eating out of my hand. He'll do anything I say." The rep later loses the customer to a competitor. Why? Because the rep stepped over the line of ethical manipulation. In an illusion of control, the rep convinced the customer to order something by overriding the customer's objections. The customer gave his authority to the rep on a previous purchase, with good results, so he does it again, succumbing to the salesperson's manipulative sales pressure. But this time the customer has some inner reservations. When the purchase does not work out, the customer becomes angry. The salesperson made the customer's judgment look bad to his boss.

The manipulative control the rep had is terminated abruptly. More important, there are hard feelings because the customer holds the salesperson and the company's sales practices responsible.

This kind of unethical manipulation works sometimes. But it frequently backfires.

A Sale Should Not Be Closed By Unethical Manipulation

Prospects may be allowed to sell themselves on the product or service. Let their image of your product evolve; then lead the prospects into a buying frame of mind. If you evaluate the prospects' needs and wants, your empathy will tell you when and how to use the various closing sales techniques to get the sale. Guard against believing you are in total control of the sales relationship or you will find yourself misleading and pressuring the prospects.

A prospect who needs or wants your product will feel good after the purchase. There will not be an aftertaste of manipulation.

But, if the prospect feels unfairly manipulated—with greed or guilt or anxiety—there will not be another order.

Trial Closing the $100,000 Movie Ticket

Let us go back to Richard the Moviemaker. Two weeks have passed since Richard sent his beautifully bound 120-page treatment of the movie story to the people he cold called. Also included was the budget for the film, financial statements of the production company, the names and resumes of the actors, the writers, and the director, and artist's renderings of a few scenes in the movie. Richard will now begin to make second calls to his prospects, intent upon closing some for a $100,000 investment in the movie production.

Richard the Moviemaker's original cold call was an attempt to find people with some fascination or interest in a movie production company. He was quite successful, coming up with fifty-six names of qualified prospects. These prospects were qualified in two areas: interest and $100,000 to invest. These prospects were put in his notebooks as Group "A" for him to follow up with a second telephone call in ten days or two weeks. He planned it this way to be sure the prospects had received his material.

In calling this group for a second time he would be aided by the material he had mailed to them. The written material would help expand the prospect's interest in the movie project.

DOS AND DON'TS ON THE TRIAL CLOSE

DO
Prepare yourself to requalify your prospect and close the sale if you can; but only if you can develop enough interest within the prospect for what you are selling.

DON'T
Talk about topics that are controversial without testing the prospect's views. Keep the conversation strictly business for the first minutes of the second call. If the prospect offers personal information accept it in a positive light. Never be critical.

DO

Move on to the next prospect if your feelings tell you the prospect is definitely not interested. Your own feelings are never wrong for you. If you are not sure about the prospect, do not directly confront his evaluation of your product or service. You must test his assertiveness by asking for suggestions on the performance of the product he would like to see or have included.

DON'T

Knock the product or service the prospect is using in lieu of yours. It makes you seem like a sore loser. Instead, point out benefits or services that your product offers.

DO

Continue your talk if in your judgment a possibility of a sale exists.

DON'T

Get involved with a "stroker." Here again, you must pay attention to your feelings for signs of your frustration to determine if you are wasting your time.

DO

Lecture the prospect after you have established your credibility. Ask her to take written notes and take on a parental authority with her by personalizing the conversation. Show her she is special by your consideration of her needs or wants.

DON'T

Ever present an illogical presentation. Skipping details can make a sales presentation confusing.

DO

Give a testimonial of your product, but make sure it is in good taste.

DON'T

Moderate your passion for what you are selling. Remember, you chose the job because the personality of the product was to your liking. It is, in fact, your child!

DO
Use inferences! They can sometimes stimulate the prospect's mind more than spoken words.

DON'T
Use inferences that are vicious or can be termed unethical manipulation.

DO
Ask for the order if you feel the lecture and testimonial have been effective.

DON'T
Be discouraged if, after the first closing attempt, the prospect says, "I want to think it over."

DO
Realize that sales resistance is at work and you must ethically manipulate your way through it just like walking through a forest.

DON'T
Get caught up in the rhythm of the prospect's questions. Answer the questions slowly with thought on your part. A question and answer rhythm is manipulation by the prospect in order for you to make an error. An analogy would be a trial attorney cross-examining a hostile witness.

DO
Draw the silent prospect out. Silence could be a tool of closing, but not at this point in the dialogue because the prospect, even though armed with some product information and knowledge, does not have enough to make the purchase decision.

DON'T
Try to metaphorically hype the prospect. It would be a disaster for it is an obvious manipulative tactic.

DO
Exert your mastery over your own actions and reactions to the prospect's utterances, not over the prospect.

DON'T
Try to be perfect. There is no such thing as perfection.

DO
Discover the prospect's hidden agenda, or the expectations from the product or service. If they are too much, modify the expectations to the reality of the product or service.

DON'T
Take advantage of the prospect's too high expectations. If you do it will come back to haunt you. You will not get reorders and you might get complaints to higher authority or even be sued.

DO
Use the tools of ethical manipulation properly. Even though they are corny and mundane, they still work.

DON'T
Get taken in by disguised sales resistance. Act according to your judgment as to whether to pursue the sale or call back another time.

DO
Act in a righteous and ethical manner. Never look to control the prospects, but rather to persuade them to buy. Always back up any promises you have made.

The Second Call Is a Sorting Call

The 120-page book that was sent to the people in Group "A" holds the key to rejection or acceptance of the proposition on the second call. Just as with a vacuum cleaner or an insurance policy or another investment, the literature is the conversation piece for the second call. It is the basis for the close. If the prospect read and liked the material, the telephone salesperson can be compared to the baseball player who just hit a single and is on first base.

The prospects in Group "A" who survive this second sorting

call or trial close will move to Group "B" for the third and final phase of the close.

In any event, Richard the Moviemaker, being the excellent telephone salesperson that he is, attempts to close on his second call if he feels the prospect is ready for it. It depends on the kind of personal connection he makes with the prospect. If he attempts to close prematurely he could blow it forever. If he lets an opportunity to close the deal pass unnoticed that would be as bad, for a second chance might not come.

To give you an idea of how the second call goes, I've set out the dialogue, taken from notes Richard made after the fact.

Important factors that you cannot perceive in this dialogue are Richard's voice inflections and his tone. Punctuation can never be the same as hearing the real conversation.

The reader must therefore call upon his imagination and ask how he would have handled the conversation:

Salesperson: Mr. Johnson, please.
Operator: One moment, please, I will transfer the call.
Secretary: Mr. Johnson's office.
Salesperson: Mr. Johnson, please—Richard the Moviemaker calling.
Secretary: What is this in reference to?

In answer to this question the mistake most salespeople selling investments make is saying: "It's a personal matter." The salesperson's meaning is the call does not pertain to Mr. Johnson's vocation. This expression should not be used, since nothing exists of a personal nature between the prospect and the salesperson at this point.

The Moviemaker Always Answers Candidly!

Salesperson: I spoke to him two weeks ago about an investment and this is a follow-up call to the information I sent him. Now, if he is very busy please don't disturb him because I would like to speak to him at length. I can

call back when he has some free time, or he can call
me back if he wishes.

The Moviemaker Qualifies the Prospect as He Speaks!

Richard the Moviemaker has taken some risks using the secretary as a messenger. He has asked her to act as a go-between. In this role she is asked to qualify Mr. Johnson's interest in the movie project for Richard and bring him back the answer. This is dangerous because Mr. Johnson's fragile interest may dissipate.

Some Prospects Can't Say No!

Because of our empathetic nature, all of us find it difficult to say "No" directly. Executives and businesspeople who can't be candid say "No" through their assistants. Telephone salespersons risk a negative reaction every time they give the secretary or assistant the purpose of the call. They make the "No" easier for the prospect because it can be delivered indirectly. This is the risk Richard the Moviemaker takes by relaying his message through the secretary. But there is a positive side as well. If the prospect has deepened his interest by reading the material, he will send some sort of positive message back through the secretary.

In this case it paid off, for Mr. Johnson picked up the telephone a few moments after Richard's message was given to him. He said to Richard: "Richard, I am quite busy now, but I read your proposal and I have a few questions. Can you call me back?"

This is the ultimate qualification and a telephone salesperson's dream prospect. The reason for the salesperson's happiness is not that he assumes he will sell the prospect, rather it is proof that the system of sorting prospects' interest through cold calling and sending written material works.

The Call Back

Mr. Johnson wanted a call back at 4:00 P.M. in the afternoon, at which time he would be free to talk about the movie investment.

Richard: [*After salutations*] Did you like the information I sent on the production, Mr. Johnson?

Mr. Johnson: Well, yes and no. It seems that this is quite an ambitious project. What make you so sure you can get it off the ground?

Richard: Mr. Johnson, my business experience has proven one thing to me. It's never the deal, it is the people in the deal that make it work, and the people in this deal have been chosen carefully for their ambition and their ability.

                 [*Richard's analogy, "It's never the deal, it's the people in the deal," is reassuring.*]

                 For example, look at the producer, Mr. Brown. He is forty-five, and look at his credits for a comparatively young man. The director is also accomplished—look at his successes. As you can see, the budget statement is certified by the accounting firm of Jones and Jones.

Without interruption, Richard the Moviemaker takes his prospect, Mr. Johnson, into the mathematics of the proposition. Facts now permeate the sale. Richard is well versed in costs, projected overruns, and reserves should unforeseen circumstances arise. This part of the conversation lasts for fifteen or twenty minutes as the men, with a copy of the budget in front of each of them, go over it line by line.

Successful Ethical Manipulation

Mr. Johnson: I don't know, Richard, the numbers sound good, but I will have absolutely no control over the money I invest.

Richard: Not true, Mr. Johnson. You are a pretty successful

fellow in your own right. We want your ideas; we want
you to get involved in the business end. Come to
Hollywood, come to the set and watch your money
work. You are going to see how much fun shooting a
movie can be as well as the lucrative return on your
investment.

[*Richard's remarks are aimed at manipulating Mr. Johnson's ego by telling him "We just don't want your money, we
want you as an intelligent, thinking person." Here we see
Mr. Johnson as a man who doesn't want to be used for his
money alone. He wants to be appreciated as a businessperson.*]

Mr. Johnson: What do you mean?

Richard: Just what I said—we want you involved! You take a
vacation during the year, don't you?

Mr. Johnson: Why, yes, of course I do!

Richard: Then plan to take it in California so you can see the
movie being shot. Besides, there is a lot to do in
California.

Mr. Johnson: [*Thinking of taking his wife to the set, and what conversations he and his wife could have at the country club over
dinner with their friends*] This all sounds good, Richard,
but $100,000 is a serious amount of money. I have to
show this proposal to my accountant and I will decide
then.

[*Richard has touched upon Mr. Johnson's hidden personal
agenda. Richard now senses Johnson's deeper interest. Richard feels Johnson is fearful of an error in his judgment. If
Richard pushes Johnson now, Johnson will rebel against his
own feelings, which have clouded his objectivity.*]

Richard: [*Taking the pressure off Johnson*] Oh, absolutely! I don't
blame you! Money is always a problem. I take risks,
too, in giving up my time when I don't really know if
the people I talk to are qualified financially. The
financial reporting services say they are, but from the
time the reporting service gathers information to the

time the investor has to write a check to the production company, things can change.

[*It seems Richard is manipulating Mr. Johnson by actually giving him a way out. Richard is saying to Johnson, "Tell me you haven't got the cash available." Richard is putting Mr. Johnson in a trap that he won't come out of without investing.*]

Mr. Johnson: [*Saying the expected*] The truth of the matter, Richard, is I am very interested in the project but my money is a bit tight. I am cash poor. I would love to get into this kind of a deal though!

Mr. Johnson thinks he is now manipulating Richard. The truth is that Johnson's sales resistance has been penetrated by ethical manipulation. He is unaware that his last statement has given Richard the avenue to pursue the close. Richard the Moviemaker has gotten what he wanted from Johnson, which is an outright admission of wanting to get into the deal, but not having $100,000 in cash at the moment to invest. Thus, the manipulation goes like this: Johnson is afraid of a new investment such as the movie; he is hesitant, yet interested, as the numbers of the deal are good. Sales resistance is fear of something new or change. Human beings resist change! But if someone reassures them by winning their confidence, then sales resistance is penetrated. The emotional benefits of interest must be admitted to by Mr. Johnson. Once he has said, "Yes, I like the whole idea," the salesperson has only to show he is a friend. Richard the Moviemaker has had a realistic financial alternative for Mr. Johnson all the time, as any friend would! Richard's experience in telephone selling told him Johnson's paralanguage has been sincere and his words meaningful.

Richard now begins the final dialogue to show Mr. Johnson an alternative financial plan, where there is a small financial outlay, and the psychological benefits as well as the money mathematics of the investment remain the same.

Richard: You know, you sound like a hell of a guy, a man who wants to contribute to the culture of America, like I do, for that is what moviemaking is! I am going to send you a package of papers for you to take to your accountant to fill out. I am going to loan you the money at a nominal rate of interest through the production company's bank. Here is how we will do it: You sign a note for $90,000 that you guarantee the bank if your financial statement warrants it. You will need about $10,000 in cash and that is all. You will still have the same equity in the production and the same benefits. We will assign the royalties from the distribution company to the bank to pay off your note so that this liability for $90,000 that you are assuming is paid off first. After the bank gets their $90,000 back that you guaranteed, you get your share of the profits along with the other investors. As you read in the proposition, XX Distributors have already guaranteed X dollars as royalties. The risk to you, of course, is how the movie attracts viewers. If it's big at the box office, we will make a lot of money. If it is not, well, at least we will get the write-off in taxes and get our money back over a number of years.

Mr. Johnson: Now that sounds good, Richard. Why don't you send it along?

[Mr. Johnson now feels that his risk is being shared and he is a special person. After all, look at what Richard is doing for him!]

Richard: I will express mail it. You will have it tomorrow!

Mr. Johnson: Sounds like it might be good, Richard. *[Mr. Johnson repeats himself again, reinforcing his deep interest to Richard.]* Send those papers. I want to look at them. But remember, I am not promising anything! *[A sign that a trace of sales resistance still remains and will hopefully be overcome on the final close.]*

Richard: Of course not. I understand that, Mr. Johnson. But keep this in mind: This is a pretty good deal and I have enough people interested at this point to have the investment shares of this particular movie sold out. So please, you sound like the kind of person I could get along with, and as I said, I would love to have you involved!

[Here we see the manipulative technique of limiting offer.]

Mr. Johnson: I will talk to you soon.
Richard: Certainly, Mr. Johnson. Goodbye for now.
Mr. Johnson: Goodbye.

The example that you have just read, although abbreviated, is ethical manipulation used professionally and wisely. Nowhere is there any misrepresentation or high pressure. Do not let any critic ever sway you from this reality of business life. As long as there is something for sale that requires dialogue, there will be manipulation on both sides of the conversation!

To sum up, there is no such thing as non-manipulative living or non-manipulative selling. That does not take away from the nobility of life or the selling profession. Rather it adds to it if one behaves as Richard the Moviemaker did—ethically putting all the facts on the table.

We shall pick up this conversation again in Part Four on closing and see how Mr. Johnson finally invests in the movie.

Ethical Manipulation at Its Best

Airline reservations people are telephone salespeople. They apply ethical manipulation techniques in such a natural way that it almost goes completely unnoticed. Their technique evaded me for a long time because they are a soft sell; the sales tactics are firm without rudeness. Airline reservations people are incoming telemarketeers, not cold callers. This is important to their concept of selling, but what concerns us is the courtesy they show to callers.

One of the things that makes the airline reservations people special is how they say "Hello." The caller dials, gets connected, and listens to the ringing of the phone. If the lines are busy, after three or four rings, a recorded message comes on to tell you either you are next or you are stacked up, just like the airplanes waiting for a turn to land. After a few moments, you are greeted by a voice identifying the agent as Miss A, Mrs. B, or Mr. C and the words,

"How can I help you?" You then state your need and off we go into the greatest ethical manipulation sales pitch.

The two underlying psychological reasons that motivate people to buy airline tickets are either "need" or "want," and the airline reservationist quickly learns which applies to the caller. The agent senses the urgency of the traveler's need or want through the inflection of the prospect's voice. Is the caller making the trip for business (a need) or a vacation (a want)? This is important to the sales agent because there are many price levels for the same ticket. Vacationers usually plan out a trip weeks or even months in advance. They always try to get the bargain fare. A businessperson, because the trips are a tax write-off, usually pays more than the vacationers because the trip can't be scheduled that far ahead, unless traveling to a convention, a sales meeting, or some other planned event.

The airline salesperson searches the computer for the specific dates the prospect wishes to travel. Then the jockeying begins for the price. A much higher price for the business traveler and a lower one for the vacationer.

The sales agents are trained to sell the seat for the top price they can get. They then stress the urgency of picking up that ticket by a specific date to keep the bargain price intact (limited offer manipulation).

If there's a problem, the computer reservations system is the villain, not the salesperson. As the information comes up on the monitor the salesperson verbalizes it. Approval and disapproval is almost instantaneous. If the telemarketer feels the prospect slipping away, back he goes to the computer, searching for comparative routes. He gives the information to the prospect and waits to hear a signal of approval. Then comes the close and the price. As I said earlier, it is always for the highest dollar amount the seats will bring. Let us call it the list price subject to discounting. If an objection comes such as:

Prospect: "But you advertised $225 round-trip in the newspaper. Why are you telling me $400 now?"

The salesperson replies without hesitation but with gentleness and confidence.

"Mrs. Jones, you are quite correct but you want to leave on

February 1, and that is six days away. We do honor the $225 fare, but those reservations have to be made seven days in advance."

Feeling manipulated by the computer, the prospect either gives in to the computer information and pays the price or simply says "forget about it." But if the salesperson hears the latter comment, he uncovers his "killer" sales closing instinct by using natural politeness. The sales agent does not forget about it! "Hold on, please," the agent says. "Let me go back into the computer and see what I can do for you." And back the agent goes, punching symbols, looking at the computer monitor intensely, vowing that this fish will not get away. You can bet that the agent will come up with something—a happy compromise, perhaps at $275 or $300 but less than the list price and more than the advertised price.

If the prospect seems to be happier with the new arrangement, the salesperson then says, "How many did you say will be traveling?" now waiting for the positive feedback.

Once booked, the sales agent asks for business and/or resident phone numbers in case of flight cancellation. Giving phone numbers serves another purpose. Psychologically it obligates the client. The sales agents' concern for comfort and safety are also always present. These empathetic expressions are another necessary part of the sales close.

Even an old pro like myself is awed by the airline marketer's class as they close their deals. Their personalities project friendliness, warmth, and concern for your comfort and safety. Starting at the full list price and moving on down in price until the prospect is convinced that she got the best fare possible is closing at its best.

There is much to be learned from airline reservations salespeople. These agents handle themselves well. They apply their ethical manipulative practices in such a natural way that it goes almost unnoticed. There is no finer example of manipulating product knowledge into sales technique.

What happens if you are not persuaded to buy the tickets? They all sign off by graciously saying, "Thank you for calling XXX Air Lines!"

Chapter 8

SALES MEETING ON TRIAL CLOSING

Question: *When you feel your prospect is receptive on the second call, should you go all the way and try to close?*

Answer: Absolutely.

Question: *Your theory about ethical and unethical manipulation is sort of way out. How did you arrive at it?*

Answer: By understanding how I manipulate people and how they manipulate me!

Psychoanalytical consultation helped me understand it on a personal basis. I applied what I learned about myself in selling and by reading two great books by C. Wright Mills, the very noted sociologist. They were *White Collar* and *The Social Imagination*.

Manipulation has replaced force in the gaining of authority over others. All forms of the media have turned very manipulative. What I have tried to point out is that if you harness this ability to manipulate others in a very ethical way it will make you a very successful telephone salesperson.

Question: *Isn't the second call or trial closing really an attempt at closing? Why do you call it a trial? The semantics gets rather confusing. I think of a trial as something where someone stands before his peers and awaits their judgment.*

Answer: You have just partially answered your own question. The telephone salesperson is before the prospect waiting for a verdict in a sense on what has been offered for sale. But the real meaning of a trial close is that the salesperson is going to attempt to close this prospect, knowing full well that it may not happen on this call. Both people, prospect and salesperson, are going to get a sample of each other's personality. The salesperson will test the prospect's sales resistance with the prospect, who, even as he resists the change a purchase or investment means to him, will get all the facts he can from the salesman. The prospect wants to settle the pros and cons of why he should or should not buy the offering. The salesperson wants the satisfaction of selling the product or service now, so both parties test each other.

Another analogy of a trial close is its likeness to the missionary work of a field salesperson. After visiting the same prospect over and over again, at some point she gives up and stops calling on that individual, or she writes up the order.

You could have three or four trial closes with a prospect, going from the lowest level of abstraction about the product or service to the highest. There is no limit to what you can say. But, a trial close is showing proof of the product's or service's performance. New proof, old proof, any proof . . . until the prospect is convinced.

Question: *Is Richard the Moviemaker doing another movie?*

Answer: Yes he is, and needless to say in Part Four I will describe how he closes his deals.

Part Four

CLOSING THE SALE

Chapter 9

BEGINNING THE CLOSE

Your first call to a prospect is a cold call because there's no emotional connection at that point between you and the prospect. Your second call—the trial close—can be termed a "warm call" because there is now a connection—the memory of the first call. Begin your closing call with a summation or recapitulation. A summation is necessary because the prospect has done one of the following since you last conversed:

- Forgotten your conversation
- Put the written material from you aside without reading it
- Quickly skimmed the written material without fully understanding it
- Carefully read the written material

If the latter has happened, the prospect is sure to have some questions to ask you.

123

Refresh the prospect's memory as to some of the important facts and points you mentioned in your previous calls. Try to recapture the prospect's old interest, but don't limit yourself to facts you've already stated. Say something new if you can to kindle new interest in your product or service.

Lay the groundwork to continue the previous phone presentation. Use words such as "very," "really," and "for sure" to intensify your statements. Speak faster than usual to project confidence. Above all, make your speech powerful by using an animated and expressive tone.

Salesperson:	Ms. Prospect, it's been three weeks since we spoke. A lot has been added in the way of benefits to that policy we spoke about on the twenty-ninth. I think it will revolutionize the disability insurance business.
Prospect:	Really?
Salesperson:	Remember I told you about how the benefits are paid immediately upon presentation of a doctor's certificate?

[*This is the beginning of the summation. Recapitulating just one fact brings back 20 percent of what the prospect previously heard. This one statement is enough of a reminder for the prospect to pick up on.*]

Prospect:	Yes, I remember that.
Salesperson:	Well, we've really gone beyond that by adding an emergency relief service that allows you to get your payments immediately by having your doctor's nurse or secretary simply phone a special number and state the facts of the illness. Of course, it must be followed up with the official certificate, but in any event the paper work begins with that very phone call, bringing your family the benefits immediately.

[*The salesperson has gone from recapitulating to new facts.*]

Prospect:	How is this verifiable? Anyone could call and say he's your doctor.

[The prospect is showing interest and wants reassurance that what she heard was correct. The salesperson perceives this interest, answers the prospect's question and then returns to his summation. The salesperson instinctively feels the timing is right to move to a close of the sale.]

Salesperson: Here's how it's done: The claims adjuster in our office asks for a phone number that can be checked in the directory, and an address, of course, and a physician's license number that can be verified with the state and hospital boards. It's really very simple when you think of it.

Ms.Prospect, our greatest attribute is simplicity in a complicated world. I think I've expressed that to you in my previous calls. As you know, we are a 100-year-old company that has never centralized. Instead we use small sales and service centers because we realize that the personal touch and caring are essential.

I think you can now see why the company received the triple A rating from the Consumer Insurance Rating Association.

I'm just thrilled with the new emergency service aspect of this policy.

After answering the prospect's question, the salesperson doesn't wait for a comment from the prospect, but instead moves quickly on into summation by repeating facts previously told the prospect. He emphasizes the benefits of quick service. He combines third-party objectivity, the information about the rating association, and evidence that he personally cares about the prospect.

During your summation be sure to speak in a confident tone. Use powerful assertive language. Make sure your voice isn't loud or high-pitched. That would negate the impression of confidence you're trying to give. It would show dependence on the prospect for the sale.

In the summation described above, the salesperson reminds the prospect of the company's service capabilities. This was described to the prospect in the second call and first mentioned during the cold call, as follows:

Good morning, Ms. Prospect. This is Mr. Sales from Love People

Insurance Company. We are a 100-year-old insurance company
with a local office here in Anytown, New Jersey. Because of our
experience and service to people we've been rated triple A by the
Consumer Insurance Rating Association, an independent consumer
watchdog organization that oversees insurance companies.

As you can see, the cold call was actually the beginning of the
close. In the closing summation we see the same statement repeated, only in a different form. In restating the theme of the first
call the salesperson has reinforced the message of service with new
information about the new emergency service added.

The summation is not the end of your attempt at closing the
sale. It's only the end of Round One. When the summation is over
you give your prospect a buying directive and try to prompt a final
judgment.

The Buying Directive

If the prospect indicates the need for more information about your
product and its benefits, give the information during your sales
presentation and summation. Answer all the questions. You're now
looking for just the right time for the buying directive.

In making your timing decision, remember that the prospect's
interest in the product is always linked to other things. Personal
problems, responsibility to a superior, and budgetary limitations all
affect the prospect's decision. If all of these factors are in order, or
set aside so they won't interfere with the decision-making, the
prospect may signal you to continue with your present course by
asking questions or for clarification of certain facts. After this is
repeated several times, you should make a judgmental statement
such as:

> "This insurance is for you, Mr. Prospect. It's everything you
> need to give you the secure feeling you need."

The prospect is being given a directive. She is being told how
she should feel about your product. Chances are she will accept
your judgment if she believes and trusts you. That's how the

unconscious mind functions for most people in a selling situation. The biggest single factor affecting whether or not the prospect will accept the directive to buy is trust in you.

Prompting a Final Judgment

After that, you must try to convince the prospect to make a final judgment. You do this by indicating that the discussion is over. It's time to act.

But you must know the prospect's nature before you try to prompt a final judgment. An immature person who looks to others to make decisions or validate decisions must be handled differently than one who makes objective decisions based on benefits versus costs.

An immature person accepts the salesperson's indirect directive "This is for you" blindly if you give the reasons to do so. If you say "your family has to be protected" you've given the immature prospect the reason to follow your directive. Most boiler rooms and telephone frauds flourish because a combination of dependent needy prospects and salespeople use distorted reasons.

Silence as a Closing Tool

Silence can be a very effective tool to close a telephone sale, but it cannot stand alone. It must be linked to other telephone sales methods, including voice, locution, and empathy.

Silence as a closing tool is not the silence produced when one party does all the talking and the other can't get a word in edgewise. Silence works as an effective sales tool when it is used after all conversation has stopped. It is the time you allow your prospect to make the buying decision.

Used this way, silence takes discipline and courage on your part. It works like this:

First, you present your sales argument, with the normal give and take of conversation. Both you and the prospect exchange personal information and you provide a full explanation of the concept of the goods or services you are selling. The prospect absorbs a lot of what is said, asks a few questions, and continues to listen.

When you sense the prospect is on the fence, ready to close, you very positively ask the magic question: "Is this product something you feel is good for you (or for your company)?

The prospect may answer positively right away, or you may get a response such as "Well-l-l-l-l . . ." and then silence for what seems like an eternity. Both you and the prospect feel the tension if you've built up your sales talk properly.

You now control the close of this sale. You can close the sale very easily or you can destroy it, depending on your reaction to the prospect's silence.

Judgment of the Meaning of the Silence

Why does the prospect grow silent at such a moment? If your sales presentation was good, it may mean the prospect is mulling your sales proposition.

Sometimes the silence is because the prospect doesn't know what to do. If you were face-to-face it would be less stressful to say "No" or "I want to think it over." Over the telephone, the prospect will instead seek or invent an interruption or a diversion—another phone call, or someone walking into the office, or even help from you.

You are also a victim of the tension in the air. In your nervousness, you may blurt out some irrelevant and untimely comment and destroy the moment.

If you have an understanding of yourself and the prospect, wait for what you feel is the right moment, and then break the silence. Give the prospect some emotional support toward an affirmative answer to your closing question. Recycle the latter part of your close—the part you feel is the most convincing part of your presentation.

Don't manipulate the prospect out of the silence by such devices as greed, guile or the like—"Your neighbors (competitors) are buying it, why don't you?" This may work for one sale, but you can never go back to the prospect again because you've exaggerated or misled. You'll get no repeat business.

However, the prospect's silence must not be allowed to last too long. A prolonged silence means the prospect's tension over the decision is about to turn into frustration. A negative answer will result.

For silence to work, timing and empathy are necessary. First, create the silence by use of a question, showing the prospect the path toward silence, and second, break the silence at the right moment with the right words.

Silence Must Be Voluntary to Be Effective

Silence only works if the prospect is allowed to withdraw into it voluntarily. If you say, "Take a few minutes to think it over," it won't work. Silence is used to give the prospect the freedom to retreat from the conversation and think. If you've presented your product well, the prospect's thoughts during the silent period are predetermined. The silence will end with either an "OK," or "I want to give it more thought."

If the prospect's response is "I want to give it more thought," don't end the conversation unless you are prepared to cast aside the time you've spent on the call. Repeat your major sales premise, support it with different minor facts you didn't mention earlier, and create a whole new conclusion having to do with reliability and confidence. Ask the prospect to see the possibilities. As a courtesy to you the prospect will become silent again while trying to visualize new thoughts.

Practice Your Own Silence in Order to Master It

Silence is easy to develop as a selling instrument. Simply go into a room by yourself and examine your feelings. Does silence make you uneasy or tense? Does it make you receptive to the next voice you hear? Study silence as you would any other subject. Used correctly it can be the most provocative closing tool there is.

DOS AND DON'TS OF CLOSING THE SALE

DO

Begin the closing call with a summation of the previous calls by going over the information previously given.

DON'T

Add more information without reviewing the old.

DO

Give more information than what you set out to give. Remember, every product or service has linkage with what surrounds its use of benefits.

DON'T

Limit your thinking. Expand on your thoughts about the product, the industry, and other factors.

DO

Direct your prospect to give you an order by asking for it.

DON'T

Ever break your prospect's mood if he is silent at this point in the sale. You are disturbing his privacy.

DO

Hold back your anxiety if it is prevalent. Turn the mouthpiece of the telephone away. Heavy breathing is a sign of nervousness, and your prospect may hear it and react negatively because of it.

DON'T

Let the silence go on too long. Use your knowledge of the prospect and your empathy to determine when he has had enough time to think things through.

DO

Gently bring the prospect out of his silence with reassuring words, not manipulative ones.

DON'T
Think you can force silence on any prospect. Your prospect must determine this for himself.

DO
Practice silence yourself to prove its effectiveness. Meditating is the form of silence I am referring to.

DON'T
Replace feeling empathetic with an intellectual process. They are two different character traits.

DO
Practice your empathy by identifying with a character in a book, a TV movie, movie or play. See if you can feel what the actor is acting out or verbalizing.

Chapter 10

THE PSYCHOLOGY OF SELLING

Psychology and selling go together. To be a successful salesperson you must understand psychology—the prospect's psychology and also your own.

When I managed the New York branch office of a national telemarketing company, I reviewed each day's work with the company president. He would end the daily review with the words, "Let's go get 'em!" I heard those words each workday for nine years.

The phrase soon lost its meaning because of the daily repetition, but it always left me with a vaguely uncomfortable feeling. It was said in a benignly aggressive tone and I sensed some hostility.

When I changed jobs, I found myself ending sales meetings with the same words, or "Hit 'em hard!" or "Charge!" as if I were a general leading my troops into battle. My words reflected my own sales aggressiveness. What I meant, at least on the surface, was "Go get some business by being aggressive."

But there was another, deeper meaning. My exhortations

reflected a kind of hostility or anger prompted by a fear of failure. They were caused by my own fear of inadequacy. And they reflected the fear everyone in the room felt. Everyone was afraid of not getting a sale and afraid of suffering the humiliation and shame of failure.

My closing comments didn't help my staff's sales effort. They amounted, in fact, to a quick fix—a shot of verbal adrenaline which produced a nervous energy based on fear of failure. As an outlet for their pent-up energy my salespeople began to talk more aggressively. Some would even lose sales as a direct result of my talk because they would push too hard.

Once I realized my closing remarks were hurting our sales efforts, I replaced them with a statement aimed at instilling pride rather than fear: "Ladies and gentlemen, let's do what we all do best—let's sell!"

Different Personalities

I have learned a lot over the years about how to sell to different people. Words are interpreted by different people in different ways. You need to use these differences to help you in your sales efforts.

First, I've seen a great difference in the reactions of men and women. Women tend to be more visual in their thoughts. A woman will generally see more "pictures" in her mind than a man would. Men, on the other hand, seem to repress their visual side when it comes to business.

Woman without business experience speak to your eye. That's also true for blue collar and service workers, male or female, because their vocabulary is limited.

Engineers are tough people to sell to for as a rule they obey known laws of space and time. If you give your sales presentation in a two-dimensional fashion, their perception makes it three-dimensional in their minds. They are, for the most part, dominated by introverted tendencies.

Businesspeople tend to speak to themselves more than to the salesperson. This means their conversation is filled with pauses. This is also true for well-educated people. Their thinking processes are more developed and their vocabularies more extensive. The silence technique can be very useful in these circumstances.

Salespeople are easily sold unless they are sales engineers. But remember that finances are always a consideration because of the highs and lows of sales.

Retail merchants are very prudent. They are, as a rule, limited risk takers. Keep in mind that entrepreneurship is encouraged in America only on the basis of new inventions, better services, and promotional material. You're more likely to be successful with a promotional item with a retail merchant if you offer to share the risks. Retailers don't like to absorb the full burden of promotional costs.

Educators are generally untrusting and nonmanipulative. The same is true of physicians and dentists. They are all in their professions because of an inability or distaste for manipulation. Lawyers, on the other hand, have a flare for manipulation. As a rule, you must dot your i's and cross your t's to successfully complete a telephone deal with a lawyer. Accountants, as might be obvious, always buy on the basis of numbers.

When you sell to senior citizens or retired persons be careful not to challenge them or try to penetrate their defenses. These people are only concerned with survival. Many are financially needy and not good prospects. Those who are well off are frequently invested or insured to the hilt. I believe they are an unlikely group for sales unless the product or service is specifically designed for their needs and wants.

Fear of Abandonment

As a supervisor of telephone sales I've seen many people succeed in telemarketing. I've also seen some failures. In many cases the person who fails at telemarketing has a personality trait or flaw that causes the failure. We can learn a lot from these failures. For that reason I will describe one of the situations, changing identifying details to protect the individuals' privacy.

Peter was a heavy-set man in his late twenties. I later learned that when Peter was a baby, his father abandoned him and his mother. As we will see, this abandonment had a strong effect on his sales ability.

Peter worked on a commission basis and when he needed money to pay his bills he was a proficient salesman. He could then close six to ten sales a day. But there was no consistency. When he didn't have a pressing financial need to make a sale, the sales just didn't come.

When a prospect refused his sales offer, Peter would go into a depression. He would sit at his desk and just stare into space for about fifteen minutes. He would then come into my office, either just to talk or to ask an insignificant question unrelated to business.

I was concerned over Peter's sales performance. I asked him to record his sales talk on tape so that I could critique his presentation and possibly help him overcome his sales problem.

This is an example of one of his conversations:

Buyer: Hello. John Buyer here.

Peter: Hi, John. Peter Walker calling. National Chemicals. How are you? Did you like our promotion on Quicksolve? Isn't that price, $80 a drum, terrific?

Buyer: Peter, how have you been? I'm doing prettty good, but business is crap. Your new deals are pretty good, I do have to admit. But with sales the way they are I'm not going to need a thing for another six to eight weeks. I'm overstocked now. Hey, Peter, did you see that Redskins game last night? Wasn't that last quarter something?

Peter: Yeh, it was a great game. John, aren't you going to need some promotions for the holidays?

Buyer: Don't think so; think I'm going to get rid of some inventory. I'll mark some good stuff down and try to move slow-moving items. Think they can catch the Giants?

Peter: Never happen. Simms is hot and the line is too strong.

Buyer: Those Skins got these two rookie receivers; they're going to make a big difference. Your Giants are going to have a tough fight this year.

Peter: It might be too late to catch them this year. The schedule favors the Giants.

I spent several days listening to Peter's tapes. A pattern began to emerge. Peter would let his emotional needs take over his sales calls. He would enter into a sales conversation, establish his credibility, "lecture" about the product and seem to be moving smoothly towards a successful close. He would then destroy all his efforts by digressing into sports talk. If the prospect digressed first Peter made no real effort to bring the conversation back to business. Sports were Peter's only outside interest in life and sports talk seemed to allow him a certain camaraderie with other men.

Near the end of his sales presentations, and faced with the close and the possibility of both rejection and termination of the phone conversation, Peter avoided both by turning the conversation to sports. In the middle of a close, when the prospect was about to say "yes" or "no" to his request for an order, I heard him say, "Do you remember that pass Namath threw against the Colts in the Superbowl?" His purpose was no longer to sell, but to be liked. Peter sought to continue the telephone relationship at any cost.

Peter's knowledge of sports and sports trivia was extensive. The prospect with an interest in sports enjoyed the conversation. Peter frequently received compliments on his sports knowledge, which encouraged his digressions. Peter would build a friendship with a prospect which he then was afraid to lose by asking for an order and being turned down. Peter unconsciously felt that if the prospect didn't place an order the relationship would be ended, and the relationship was too important to Peter to risk.

Peter had lost his sense of business purpose. He controlled the conversation, but not for the right reason. He made a good connection with the prospect in the give-and-take about sports. This could have been used to make the transition to business and then to close the sale. Instead, Peter made his sales calls into social calls.

What should he have done instead? When Peter found out that the buyer would be ready to buy in six to eight weeks, he should have set up a time for a recall. When the buyer brought up football, Peter's initial response was good: He moved the conversation back to business. But when the buyer brought up sports again, Peter should either have politely cut the conversation short, so he could make a new call, or he should have offered to help the buyer by suggesting some ways to get rid of the overstocked inventory. This would have demonstrated Peter's business expertise and would have created good will. It would have insured a good reception when Peter called for a new order.

To be effective in telephone sales you must set aside your own emotions. Making sales should make you feel good. Don't lose the focus of your sales talk by injecting your own emotional needs into it. The purpose of the call is to sell. Stick to that purpose and you'll be successful.

Chapter 11

ACCEPTING
PEOPLE'S VOICES

Accepting people's voices is a substitute for accepting their physical appearance.

I find that gathering a little bit of personal information beforehand is a useful tool in accepting my prospect's entire demeanor. I learn about character from words and paralanguage. It awakens my empathy and gives me a better understanding of the prospect. Once I establish that the prospect is the kind of person to whom I could be a friend, I form a relationship by voice alone.

Now, of course, with some people it is strictly business. If they make money with me they stay; if they suffer one loss, that is the end of the relationship. I know these people so well that if I hear anger in their voices, I ask them if they are angry at me. Some are reluctant to tell me they are mad at me for possibly giving a wrong recommendation. I feel a certain amount of sadness that complicates some of my relationships when people whom I care about suffer a financial loss. But I never avoid bringing up their feelings. I literally force them to verbalize their feelings. In this way no one harbors a grudge.

I am human, and as a human, I am subject to making errors in judgment. I get this point across to my prospects and clients by giving them information about my personal life. I get back information about their lives. I know how far they can go financially, if they love their wives or husbands, their problems with their in-laws and children; but this type of personal information comes only with certain personality types and only after they become clients. I care about their money and I care about them, and they hear the sincerity in my voice.

I wrote earlier that manipulation is a tool to penetrate sales resistance. I also stated that manipulation could not be used to close. Closing requires a connection. That connection to help you close must be empathetic in nature.

My personal selling experience in telephone marketing has been varied. Home improvements, chemicals, investments, real estate, photographic equipment, mortgages, and frozen foods, just to name a few. But this philosophy fits every item or service for sale. Establishing a prospect voice acceptance pattern in yourself will open up your intellectual and empathetic capacity to give to others and to take for yourself. Both of these attributes must be at work at all times to close sales.

Empathetic Listening

Empathy is the ability to put yourself in the prospect's position. Once this identification takes place, you become the problem-solver for the moment, for you gain an understanding of the prospect's thinking. The prospect's problems could range from no confidence or interest in the product that you are selling to lack of finances or time to talk to you. There are any number of different things that could prove negative.

But empathetic listening is not just a tool for receiving negative input from a prospect. It is also a positive means of communication. It is a connecting device, the coupling between people in everyday affairs. Empathy could also be the connection between what an

DOS AND DON'TS ON ACCEPTING PEOPLE'S VOICES

DO
Gather useful personal information about your prospects so you can determine if they think in pictures or just abstract thoughts.

DON'T
Project the image of an adversary on your prospects. Try to be a good friend.

DO
Draw out your prospects. Reassure them they won't lose you if they get angry at you for some reason.

DON'T
Avoid your anger or bad feelings either. Keep the relationships honest.

DO
Care about your clients' money as you would your own. Give them the best deal or the best price you can.

DON'T
Hurt yourself by doing the above.

DO
Try to make each business relationship a special one.

DON'T
Ever take the attitude your prospects or clients are out to do you in. If this is true, cease doing business with them.

DO
Accept a prospect at his word. Don't read a special meaning into it by telling yourself he didn't mean it or he meant something else.

individual thinks of as shameful and guiltful actions and reactions to others and himself. When we have done something for no apparent realistic reason, all of us have said to ourselves, at one time or another, "I don't know why I did that." It is with the use of our empathy that we forgive ourselves. We remember the time, the place, the circumstances of the once unpardonable incident and could say, "I did it because I was frightened." This is the act of self forgiveness brought about because we identified with ourselves in the past and remember those feelings and their causes in the present.

So, empathy must come from listening, not only from listening to others, but to our own thoughts. Our individual feelings never betray us. Our feelings separate fact from fantasy, truth from fabrication, and sincerity from manipulation by others.

In sales, the use of empathy provides answers to questions such as: "Is this person who answered the CEO's telephone the CEO or an underling?" "Is this customer a stroker or sincerely interested in my product?" "Does this person mean he does not have the purchase price of the sale item or is it a manipulative effort to bow out of the conversation gracefully?"

Only your empathy stimulated by your feelings can tell you the answer to these questions. You must learn to listen attentively, first to the prospect, and then to yourself, to fully develop your empathy.

On the other side of the empathetic coin is the response that stimulates positive feelings. Our empathetic thoughts could go like this: *This person's confidence must be built up once or twice more, and then I will attempt to close this deal. Or he is on the fence—let me instigate some silence so this prospect can think through my point of view for a few moments.*

These are the judgments with which the salesperson moves into the dialogue smoothly, for your empathy tells you when to speak, what to say, and when to listen.

Dialogue

Words can call people into action, manipulate them against their will, anger them, or describe the product properly or improperly. They can also literally destroy good feelings or build them.

The proper use of words put into a dialogue between salesperson and prospect creates commerce and causes the exchange of money. In short, words and their usage in sales presentations close the sale. Here again, we have linkage between personality factors in the form of the prospect's and the salesperson's perception of what they hear from each other, how they feel when they hear each other's utterances, and whether they trust what they perceive to be each other's feelings.

Empathy is the key to understanding the prospect from the telephone salesperson's point of view. There is no counter empathy. The only question is "What's in it for me?" This prevails in the prospect's mind. The prospect only thinks of "gain" in some form, be it monetary, social, emotional, or convenience.

If the prospect wants the product or service and openly admits wanting to own it, and there are no insurmountable realistic problems such as financing and delivery dates, all is well and good. But that is a rare moment indeed in business. Chances are most prospects will be hesitant or reluctant to spend their money without proof or at least trust in the salesperson. Possibly they will need a consultation with the spouse or boss or supervisor, or even a day or two to think it through, before a salesperson gets an answer. To separate the realistic problems of the prospect from possible sales resistance takes selling skill.

How to Tell the Difference

Manipulation to penetrate sales resistance of the prospect on the trial close is easily done and goes unnoticed for the relationship is new to both parties. Salesperson and prospect jockey for a comfortable position from which to relate. They feel each other out, probing for some level of confidence in each other. The salesperson looks for serious interest; the prospect, having the need or want for the product, looks to feel assurance and guidance in the salesperson's voice. A prospect with a nonmanipulative personality will move away from an overly manipulative salesperson. These prospects might not be able to describe their reactions but they will not allow anyone to make a decision for them.

Manipulation is a form of making decisions for people, of getting other people to do things against their will that serve special interests of others. Manipulation is a substitute for the direct confrontation of authority. It is done, of course, with words and dialogue and those words need not necessarily be metaphors or buzz words.

Intellectual and Emotional Stimulation in Good Dialogue

Listening to another party and using your empathy go together just as when you are reading a book and listening to the author's words within yourself. If it is a well-written book, you will really enjoy it for it makes you feel! Feeling sorry for yourself is another example of listening and feeling at the same time. You go over the event in your mind and sadness takes hold of you. Maybe you cry, maybe you feel a listlessness, but in any event the two personality traits of feeling and thinking come together.

Using the Same Devices in Sales

In sales we combine these two facts of human existence just as we do in everyday life. A telephone salesperson must develop feeling and thinking capacity by listening and letting what he hears effect his feelings. By listening, feeling, and thinking, he can judge his prospects' heights of interest so he can close the sale. If he does not consider his prospect worth listening to, then he is not a salesperson. If he speaks without using empathetic listening, then he is a locomotive thundering down the tracks at 500 miles an hour, hoping to find a prospect who will be coerced by the salesperson's assumed authority.

This type of salesperson never listens. Other people's feeling and needs make no difference, only his neediness is at stake. He has no empathetic capacity.

Let me relate a personal experience I had with such a salesperson. I was visiting my brother-in-law and sister in Hollywood,

Florida, in the winter of 1987. They had gone out to dinner and I preferred to stay at home working on some office reports due the next day. The phone rang and I answered. Before I knew it, I was mistaken for my brother-in-law and I was being pitched on a commodity investment. The broker, Miss X, was quite efficient in giving me all the facts about coffee in Brazil that were relevant to her proposition, and why coffee would go back up to the $5 a pound in price it was in 1978 and 1979.

I listened for awhile and, needless to say, I refused her offer. It was then she inundated me with metaphoric phrases and analogies. Her closing effort went like this:

Salesperson:	Mr. Nemerson, more money is lost through indecision than by making the wrong decision.
Response:	I don't see the logic behind that statement.
Salesperson:	I will put it to you another way—before your ship can come in, it has to leave the port.
Response:	But I don't want to buy a ship.
Salesperson:	[*Beginning to be confused by my manner*] Imagine, Mr. Nemerson [*even though I told her earlier that I wasn't he, she kept calling me by my brother-in-law's name*], that your cruise ship is leaving the port. Book your cabin now or swim out to the ocean trying to catch it. Which is better?
Response:	Do you mean if I send you $2,000 to invest in coffee, I will be booking a cabin on a cruise ship? I would have to do it that way [*send the money*]. I can't swim.
Salesperson:	[*Mistaking my last remark for interest because she did not listen with her feelings*] Ben Franklin always drew a line down a page. He put the pros and cons on either side of the line. If the pros outweighed the cons, he went for it.
Response:	Seriously, I don't want a history lesson nor do I want to waste your time. I am really not interested in this kind of investment.
Salesperson:	[*Once again paying no mind to my remarks*] Everyone is afraid of the dark, scared of the unknown, and fearful of anything new or different. I want you to know that I understand your feelings and reservations because they are natural. I run up against it every day with new clients. I run up against something else, and this is a phone call saying thank you for helping us get started on the path to profits!

I'm going to reach out my hand across the miles and I want you to take it. I'm going to hold your hand, advise and guide you, and lead you on the path to riches.

Response: *[In a stern voice, for now I was becoming angry for her persistance was obnoxious]* Look, I told you I wasn't interested. I don't invest in that kind of thing!

Salesperson: *[Going right on as if I didn't exist]* I can't blame you for having a little bit of doubt, a little bit of concern, and some uncertainties. That's natural. So I'm not expecting you to fearlessly jump into this. Just give me one percent of your confidence and allow me to earn the other 99 percent by making money for you.

[I knew I had the right to hang up the phone and yet I didn't. This fact was more interesting to me than the salesperson's closing attempts using her metaphoric analogies. Why wasn't I hanging up? The answer came to me in a flash. It was the lack of recognition, her failure to recognize my authority in this conversation. She just wasn't listening to me, as if I were a child whose answers didn't matter. That made it interesting. Here was this beautiful voice that had laid down some very interesting facts about a frost in Brazil and the coffee sellers getting together in a cartel to get more for their product, but yet she had no harmony in her delivery. Not listening emphatically, she could not judge the right words or facts to use. Therefore, she lost the interest I did have at the onset of the talk.]

Response: *[In a firm but serious tone]* Miss X, I really am very busy, and I want to thank you for your time, but let me repeat— I am really not interested.

Salesperson: Mr. Nemerson, you deserve this investment potential. The sooner you get started the sooner you may start making money. Putting it off could mean paying more for it. Getting started now could mean greater profits. Ninety-nine percent of investors need help making a decision. How can I help you make the right decision?

Response: *[Sarcastic tone]* You can't!

Salesperson: *[Her tone is now desperate. She heard my answer, but denied the feeling it gave her]* Mr. Nemerson, the meaning of procrastination is living yesterday, avoiding today, ruining tomorrow. Only 5 percent of the people in the world are leaders, and 95 percent are followers. The leaders are the astute investors who can size up an opportunity and make a decision based on good common sense and logic. The followers are those poor people who continually procrastinate and sit on the side lines waiting until something happens that causes the price to shoot up. Then they rush to the phone and stand in line with the rest of the followers and pay a higher price. I'd like to think that you're a leader who can see the advantages of getting started now so that you're at the front of that line watching your profits soar. This could be the best investment decision you've ever made and I know you'll enjoy the financial freedom it may give you.

This woman was now comical to me. I began to laugh and even though I put the receiver and mouthpiece of the phone a few inches away from my face, the laughter was so spontaneous and so hearty, she heard. The message that my laughter sent was very clear to her. She could no longer deny my feelings about her pitch, so she hung up.

My thoughts ran like this: She had acted like a fool. My feeling provoking the laughter were these: Here was a middle-aged man writing a book on telephone sales urging salespeople to be creative and conscientious and to understand and serve those they sold. All these positive and ethical factors were unknown to this salesperson. Her final remarks assured me that she was reading from a script, never once even understanding by the use of her own feelings the metaphors and analogies she was verbalizing. She was, in effect, mouthing words, never listening to me and counting on her authoritative tone of voice to close the sale.

My empathy told me my welfare was of no concern to her even though she said it was. How could I tell? The lack of harmony between her failure to listen to me was evident in her speech. At no time did she try to develop my interest when I said I had none. Nor did this woman cherish her own dignity. When I answered sarcastically, why didn't she call me to task by telling me I was out of place with my remarks?

An event took place months later to cap this encounter. On

another trip to Florida, over coffee one morning, I opened the newspaper. The lead story was about the Commodity Futures Trading Commission trying to close down the company that this woman who had called me represented. The reasons the CFTC gave were the following:

- High-pressure sales
- Exaggerated returns on investments
- Salespeople were urged to generate commissions regardless of the customer's risks

To paraphrase a famous television personality, "And so it goes!"

A Cameo on Successful Empathetic Listening

The following is taken from transcripts of another experience I had with a telephone salesperson. This salesperson was fully equipped with empathy and understanding as well as compassion for people's problems which resulted in a dialogue that convinced me to buy from her.

One night as I sat writing at my kitchen table, the phone rang, and I answered.

A woman's voice inquired: "Is this Mr. Novich? Mr. Martin Novich?"

Response: Yes, it is.

Woman: Am I disturbing you? If I am, I'm sorry.

Response: No . . . no, you're not. What can I do for you?

Woman: I'm Miss T from C&T Decorators. I got your name awhile ago from Welcome Wagon, which is an organization that refers people who have just moved into the neighborhood to various business and merchants that are available to them. I have been trying to contact you for the longest time without success.

Response: We're not here much. In fact, I wouldn't be here this evening but I had some work to do. In any event, if you want to sell me something I am not a good prospect. There is only my

son and me, and we are really not concerned with home
decorations.

Miss T: I detect a chauvinistic attitude in your voice. It seems to me
you have the old line attitude that interior decorating is work
for women only. Why, more men are decorators than women!
I'll bet you don't have any drapes or curtains or even carpeting.

Response: [*Ashamedly*] I do have carpeting.

Miss T: [*Laughing*] Then it had to come with the apartment! Am I
correct?

Response: [*With laughter*] How did you know?

Miss T: Because I have a lot of experience with people and you had
all the signs of bachelorhood. Some men who live alone
really don't pay attention to making a home for themselves.

[*Now I was tremendously interested in this woman's approach.
Everything that I was trying to teach about telephone cold
calling seemed to be understood by her. But I was not sure, so
I began to test her.*]

Response: Tell me, what are the signs of bachelorhood? How did you
know?

Miss T: First, it is the card I got from Welcome Wagon which read,
Mr. Martin M. Novich—"Mrs." was missing on the title.
Next, it's the location and the type of home—a condominium
development, not a house. Thirdly, I have been trying to
contact you intermittently from 10 A.M. through 5 P.M. at
least every other week, at first. Then as time dragged on, once
a month. Still no answer. Wouldn't you deduce from these
facts that this was a busy person who lived alone?

Response: You are very observant and so far, have proven yourself
perceptive. Yes, I am a bachelor but what I meant when I said
I am not a good prospect is that I am never here to look at
samples or go to furniture stores. I just haven't got the time!

Miss T: Oh, I know the story with you bachelors! And men like you
are my specialty. I will work with your schedule and all you
have to do is fill out the questionnaire that I will mail to you.
Give me the square footage for the apartment and the layout
of it in a sketch in the space provided on the questionnaire.
Include dimensions of windows and doors and sketch in the
position of the furniture. Also give the color of each room.

[*I was once again astonished by this woman's organization.
How she was trying to put me to work in a cooperative effort
and yet save me time!*]

Response: What do I do then, mail it to you?

Miss T: That's correct, and I in turn will mail you back a big brown
envelope with my recommendations listed and a book of
material swatches. Look them over and, if you will kindly give
me your telephone number at work or tell me when you are
sure to be home, I will call you and then we'll go over it
together. By the way, before I go further with this free
planning, let me assure you that this company has been in
business since 1948, is well capitalized, and I will give you
references in your area of work that we have done for other
people. Hopefully, if and when we can do some work for you,
you will allow us to use your home as a reference in the
future.

[*My thoughts about this woman were all positive. Confident
voice, empathetic, mature, assuring me of her understanding.
I liked the whole picture. Through her approach, she was slowly
turning a want into a possible need. But still, I had some
reservations.*]

Response: I am very impressed with all of this, Miss T., but tell me how
could someone be accurate about this kind of work without
seeing the place? We can't do this by telephone, and certainly
having no mechanical ability, I won't be able to hang drapes.

Miss T: Oh, Mr. Novich, pardon me when I call you naive. Of course
we can't do a job like yours without looking at it! And we
wouldn't even attempt that. But this is the preliminary planning. Planning takes up more time than anything else. If we
did this on a one-to-one, in-home basis, we would have to
have someone out to your place three or four times or maybe
more. Doing things this way, we don't take up your time, for
after I receive back your sketch and your choice of colors, and
other information about the apartment, I can give you an
approximate estimate of the cost. If that fits your priority, one
of our salesperson designers will come out to see you. If you
can't make it during the week, they will make an appointment

for Sunday or Saturday morning at your earliest convenience. But first, I want to qualify the cost to you for turning your apartment into a home!

How could I say no to such a proposition as this? This salesperson had taken every phase of my needs into consideration. My time was her first consideration, and certainly my feelings and thoughts about interior decorating were another. She assumed because of her empathetic nature that I would respond positively to her caring attitude, and she was right. I did! I was following her lead!

Never did she take control over my reactions nor did I feel any anger or resentment of being manipulated. I did it all voluntarily after she manipulated me at the onset of the conversation.

The end result? I own a new couch and drapes and have beautiful curtains on the windows. My apartment is now a home! I thank Miss T. for pursuing me as she did!

DOS AND DON'TS OF THE PSYCHOLOGY OF SELLING

DON'T
Be motivated by a fear of failure. Motivate yourself by a sense of accomplishment and the money you will *earn*.

DO
Realize the difference in the personalities of your prospects.

DON'T
Digress from the purpose of selling your product or service in your conversation with the prospect.

Chapter 12

"MAY I CALL YOU PARTNER?"

A veteran salesperson who read a rough draft of the story of Richard the Moviemaker before publication said: "Novich is all wet." It's greed that must be sold! Mr. Johnson wants money for his money. Others said Johnson wants entertainment or prestige. Another person said he is just interested in the tax shelter aspect.

Each person who commented found a different interpretation of the formula costs = benefits = happiness (first described in the Introduction) at work. The truth is that happiness is so intangible and so elusive that there just isn't an interpretation.

Unless you have an intimate sense of another person, you do not know what will make that person happy. In telephone selling, you can only tell by the prospect's verbal reactions to what you say.

The return and the shelter aspect belong in the benefits side of the equation. The greed, entertainment, and prestige belong on the happiness side.

As we shall witness, Richard the Moviemaker faces many

151

obstacles in the attempt to sell Mr. Johnson. To get Mr. Johnson to invest $100,000, Richard must apply all the lessons we have previously learned. Richard will use them in the closing attempt as the presentation demands. They are:

- Wanting and waiting
- Ethical manipulation
- Getting by the secretary
- Celebrity endorsement
- Doing favors/limiting the offer
- Credibility closing with silence

The C-B-H Formula in Use

We pick up from the second call. The prospect made an open admission of interest in the movie project.

Richard the Moviemaker was to mail documents to the prospect for him to pass on to his accountant and lawyer for study. Richard had had his last conversation with Mr. Johnson ten days ago.

Richard suggested that since Mr. Johnson expressed an interest in joining this limited partnership, but was low on cash, that Richard would arrange a loan through a reputable major New York City bank. The loan would be secured by a million dollar distribution contract from a major movie distribution company.

The financial risk was that if the film did not go over at the box office, there would be no royalties for Mr. Johnson and the other partners to share. They would have to suffer the loss.

Preparing to Close Mr. Johnson

It is 11 A.M. on Monday morning. Richard the Moviemaker sits at his desk and thumbs through his notebook. There are three sheets of paper behind his notebook paper divider that says on June 18 all prospects are to be closed that day. It is the third call for all of them. The first prospect sheet bears the name Ronald Johnson. Richard scanned the sheet in a downward glance past the personal and business information written down about his conversation with Ronald Johnson. He sees that he cold called Mr. Johnson on June 2 and the 120-page prospectus about the movie was mailed to Johnson's home. According to his notes, on June 9 he spoke to Mr. Johnson at 4 P.M. Richard's written comments remind him that the call lasted 33 minutes and the notes reflect that the talk was very positive.

The last of Richard the Moviemaker's written sentences are the most hopeful and stimulating to Richard. They read:

"Mr. Johnson admitted interest and wants to take papers to accountant and lawyer. I left him with a full feeling about the project."

Another sentence reads:

"June 9 prospect was mailed documents including subscription agreement and financial statement forms. Sent him video tape cassette of scene from the move narrated by Mr. S, a Hollywood personality."

For the third time Richard the Moviemaker dials Mr. Johnson's office. The receptionist answers.

Richard replied politely "Mr. Johnson's office, please." The extension telephone rings and now a familiar feminine voice answers for the third time: "Mr. Johnson's office."

Richard: This is Richard the Moviemaker calling. Is Mr. Johnson available?
Secretary: Oh yes. This is Mr. Johnson's secretary. Mr. Moviemaker, he's on the line. I know who he's talking to. He'll only be a few moments. Would you care to wait?
Richard: Not at all if it's only a few moments.
Secretary: No, it won't be long. Are you the man who is producing the movie I've heard him talking about? By the way, my name is Pauline, Mr. Moviemaker. This movie business sounds so exciting. I was telling my husband the other night that if we had investment money, I'd like us to invest in it.

Richard's intuition tells him that Pauline has access to some background information about Mr. Johnson's interest in the deal that would help him button up this investor. In order to find out what help she can give that he can utilize, he nurtures her enthusiasm about what she would do if she had money to invest. Richard's interest is in Mr. Johnson's investment, not his secretary! Richard hopes the secretary will take the messenger role again. "It's a limited partnership. It's just about fully sold out." (It is far from sold out, but it relieves the secretary of frustration.) Richard begins his probe of Pauline very obliquely, keeping what appears to be his attention on the secretary, but hiding what he really wants, and that is more information on Johnson's interest.

Secretary:	Well, we couldn't have done anything anyway.
Richard:	I promise you this much, Pauline, if you give me your home name and home address you can have a half dozen tickets to the premiere of the movie when we have one in your area.
Secretary:	Oh, thank you, but you don't have to do that.
Richard:	[*He is encouraged because Pauline begins to draw closer. If Johnson can only stay on the phone doing his business a few more moments, Richard will have more information.*] I suppose your boss sparked your movie madness.

[*Richard chuckles as he says that. The remark does not appear insulting.*]

Pauline:	Oh yes. Confidentially, Mr. Moviemaker, he and his wife have been talking on the telephone about the movie for days. They have a daughter, you know, at Yale, studying drama.

Richard digests that information with a gulp. It is good stuff for closing but he must be careful how he uses it. He cannot jeopardize Pauline's confidence, nor can he mention any of this to Mr. Johnson, for it would be a betrayal of Pauline. If the deal does not close on this telephone call, he may have to call a fourth time or possibly a fifth. If that turns out to be the case, enlisting Pauline's aid would be helpful. Richard will have to decide on how the conversation with Johnson goes, whether to make other calls to him should this one fail. This call will depend on how well the videocassette went over with Mr. Johnson and if the subscription document was well received by Johnson's lawyer and accountant.

In any event, Richard is prepared to wait for his closing opportunity while supplying more information pertaining to the deal, and supplying more rhetoric if need be. Why? Because he wants a $100,000 sale! The price Richard may possibly pay is waiting! A real professional does not mind waiting, because to push his prospect prematurely might kill whatever chance he has of closing a $100,000 sale. His prospect might rebel against the immediate pressure. Richard does not know the prospect well enough to know how he will react to sales pressure. Neither does Richard stereotype his prospects. He classifies prospects as introverts and extroverts, and men and women, and as to their educational and job backgrounds categories.

This gives him an edge in dealing with his prospects, but he also respects people's uniqueness within these groups. Why does a telephone salesperson such as Richard the Moviemaker do this?

As in any telephone sales presentation, the salesperson must describe his deal (or what he is selling). He must try to make the intangible tangible. He must strive to bring his idea alive! But there is danger in this and the danger is to make the proposition so good it becomes unbelievable. With words, the sound of his voice, and the force of his personality, Richard is breathing life into a movie project that is only a dream on paper at the present time. An analysis of his prospect helps to answer the big question of how can he convince this prospect to see his dream of this movie become reality? The prospect does not necessarily have to see this project in the same perspective as Richard does. He could want different results for himself. For example, Richard saw this movie as a vehicle to fulfill his personal dream of wealth. Pauline saw it as a way of bringing excitement into her life. How would Mr. Johnson see it? Only in the perspective of return and investment? Prestige? Excitement for him and his family? What was Johnson's hidden agenda? Certainly Pauline's agenda was exposed and so was Richard's. It would be a rarity indeed if Mr. Johnson did not have a hidden agenda in pursuing the project this far. Could Johnson's daughter's pursuit of an education in drama at Yale be the necessary ingredient to close the deal?

If this is so, then she (the daughter) must have been consulted. How much influence does she have in her father's decision? Richard cannot afford to make any assumptions, he must trust his feeling based on what Johnson says to him.

Richard: [*To Pauline, downplaying the importance of the information, so he would not be obligated to her*] I don't think that the fact makes much difference to Mr. Johnson; I don't know your boss that well, but it would seem to me a successful man like he is more interested in return on investment?

Pauline: Well, Mr. Moviemaker, I love your proposition, but his daughter and his wife are just as interested as he is. I know his wife copied a whole section of the book you sent and mailed it down to Connecticut to Susan. That's their daughter's name.

[*Richard's thoughts now go like this: "I must now convince Mr. Johnson and his four advisors: his accountant, his lawyer, his wife, and his daughter. The accountant and lawyer will be easy; the relatives—I don't know."*]

Pauline: Oops, he's off the phone. I'm going to switch you. Nice talking to you, Mr. Moviemaker, and I'll drop you a note about my address so you'll know where to send those premiere tickets!

Richard: Thank you, Pauline, and please do that. The address is on the cover of the prospectus.

[*Richard hears a click and a short electronic sound and the voice that answers is Mr. Johnson's. Apparently Pauline has announced Richard's call, for Mr. Johnson begins very cordially.*]

Johnson: Richard, how are you?
Richard: Fine, Mr. Johnson, for an old man.
Johnson: You don't sound so old.
Richard: Forty-four on my next birthday, which is in December. As they say, that ain't young!
Johnson: What should I say? I'm fifty-six, stopped smoking five years ago, and feel fit as a fiddle.
Richard: God, Mr. Johnson, how I've tried to stop and just can't do it. It's not that I don't want to stop. I desperately do, what with the horror stories I hear. But it's the people around me—everybody smokes and that makes it tough. Anyway, how did you like that cassette I sent along? Did you view it?

For the first time in three conversations, the men have ex-
changed free information about themselves. They are comfortable
with each other at this point. These everyday remarks are a vital
part of any sale. When and at what juncture a free information
exchange occurs is anybody's guess. Both people must be open and
ready for it. If Mr. Johnson had not been as cordial as he was,
Richard would not have offered the free information about his age.
Richard liked Johnson's greeting and connected with it. Johnson
sent back a similar cordial remark, his age, which is a common
topic for people from mid-life on. This is a subject one person can
share with another. Then the men got into smoking and health,
once again a problem discussed by people of all age groups. These
are remarks of a somewhat personal nature breaking through the
formal business barriers.

Johnson: Yes, I have, and I have to compliment you. It is good
promotional stuff, but to me it had no more impact than
a TV commercial.

*[Feeling that Mr. Johnson's interest has leveled off and is
now ambiguous, Richard moves to reawaken it by taking
the prospect back to the part of the sales presentation that
has passed, but he must do it smoothly so it is unnoticed
by Mr. Johnson. He therefore begins his summation.]*

Richard: That tape was not meant to have an impact on a sophisticated person like yourself. I don't know if you are aware of
the fact that the average movie goer has a psychological
age of fifteen years. Ours is the kind of story that the mass
of movie goers respond to. A good drama with a complicated plot belongs on public TV or on Broadway. Let me
ask you what movie in the last five years impressed you
most?

Mr. Johnson: Why I think that story about the boxer; I think it was
called—The Rage—*Raging Bull*—yes—yes that was it,
with that wonderful actor Robert DeNiro!

Richard: Ah yes. Why that one? Was it the acting? Are you a fight
fan? Or was it the story line?

Johnson: I don't know. I suppose it was the story.

Richard: Exactly. It was a wonderful story and a true one, but it was
not a money-maker at the box office. The true life figure
whose life it was based on was well known and remembered by some middle-aged people on the East Coast, and
it did well at the box office there, but that's about it. Ours
is entirely different. It was made for the masses who reside
everywhere, East, West, North, and South. There are
many ways for us to make a profit and that is what we're
after. *[Richard now is heavily into the summation.]* Remember our prospectus told you that we had more than
one market. They are the domestic market, video tapes,
international markets, and cable companies. *[Richard goes
on to summarize the entire projected sales figures and
budget costs and Mr. Johnson participates fully.]*

Johnson: My accountant and lawyer seem to feel that it will not lose
any money, but they don't seem to be sure that it will
make any either.

Is this the truth or is Mr. Johnson downplaying his
enthusiasm for tactical purposes like getting a better deal
if there is one?

Richard: *[Now goes into a testimonial about his product]* All we
need, Mr. Johnson, is to be successful in one of the four
markets that I listed for you. Mr. Johnson, I've read many
a script and all I can tell you is I chose this one to get
involved in because I felt it is the finest entertainment
piece I've read. The story will sell because it's simple and
it's fantasy. It's an escape from the realities of the computer
monitor and the assembly line and the TV set for the
average person. The average youngster and young adult
doesn't want to see life's problems, as you and I want to. I
loved *Raging Bull* for at my age I could identify with the
hero's struggle, but only because I am at a certain stage of
my life.

*[Richard's suspicions are Mr. Johnson's dampened enthu-
siasm has been caused by his daughter and his wife, who
are interested in drama. This musical, which is a fantasy,
is not to their liking. These ideas, if you remember, came
as a result of his conversation with Pauline while he was
waiting for Mr. Johnson to pick up the telephone. If this is
the final resistance to the close, it is in Mr. Johnson's*

hidden agenda. He must be made to speak about it so Richard can deal with it. Richard continues the dialogue, trying to infer that he, Mr. Johnson, has been influenced.]

Richard: You know, a very good friend of mine who is a dramatic actor scoffed at me for undertaking this musical project. His real purpose was his own interest. He wanted me to raise financing for something he could do. You know I absolutely refused! My purpose for my investors is profit.

[Here we see a combination of establishing credibility, ethical manipulation, and the inference that the same thing could be happening to Mr. Johnson at the hands of his wife and daughter. That's because their interest lies in drama. The pursuit of their happiness was interferring with a potentially profitable business deal. For the interference, too, is Richard's credibility. The credibility is inferred by the fact that he disregarded a friend's ambition and was interested in his investor's financial survival. The manipulative effort is to make Mr. Johnson speak out, telling if his family is influencing him.]

Mr. Johnson: I sort of have the same problem. My daughter, you know, is a drama student.
Richard: Oh, how nice!
Mr. Johnson: Both she and my wife feel that if I am going to invest in a movie situation, it should be a drama to help give my daughter a start in her career.
Richard: May I ask what year of school she is in?
Mr. Johnson: Why she's in her second.
Richard: Oh, I see! *[His voice tone is low and subdued as if to carry a message in paralanguage of disapproval. Once again Richard has used inference as his tool of ethical manipulation, with the tone of his voice.]*
Mr. Johnson: Is something wrong?

[Johnson's paralanguage is fraught with quiet and a slight embarassment as the realization comes over him that he is using a sophomore in college as an excuse for him to stay out of a deal that could bring him profit and personal

prestige. He is exaggerating. He doesn't know it, but Johnson is in the process of being manipulated out of his final resistance to this deal.]

Richard: [*Seizing the moment*] Nothing is wrong, for I would not comment on your personal life, but one cannot look at these business situations from an emotional point of view. Let me ask you quite frankly, is this the only reason you are hesitating? You stated your accountant and lawyer were reasonably satisfied. Mr. Johnson, I have my own money in this project. I am one of the partners also, and I want your permission to call you partner.

Johnson: Call me anything you want, but you see my problem. I can't go against the wishes of my family.

Richard: [*In a paternalistic tone*] Mr. Johnson, my question to you is simply: Has this proposition met the approval of your hired professionals, your lawyer and your accountant?

[*Richard refuses to be manipulated by Mr. Johnson to drop the whole idea of the investment in the movie.*]

Johnson: Yes it has.

Richard: Then I shall do this for you. I will use whatever influence I can to get your daughter an agent when she graduates school, but that is two years away. Why would she want to go into something now when she isn't ready?

[*Richard is doing Mr. Johnson a favor. That is acceptable manipulative selling.*]

Johnson: It wasn't her idea, it was my wife's.

Richard: Then explain this situation to your wife. Your daughter would be making a big mistake, more harmful than positive.

Mr. Johnson: I think you're right.

Richard: And you would be making a mistake by not getting into this venture.

Mr. Johnson: May I call you partner?

Suddenly the satellite that carries the electronic impulses ceases to code and decode human utterances. Both men grow silent. There is not a sound from Richard's base in Los Angeles, movie center of the world. The office of Mr. Ronald Johnson, President of BBY Company, Boston, also reflects silence as he holds the receiver to his ear.

Richard closes his eyes and imagines the distance between Los Angeles and Boston. He sees himself on an airplane on a clear day 20,000 or 30,000 feet up in the sky. The painted desert, the Rocky Mountains, Death Valley, and below him, the drowning of the jet engines are muffled as the imaginary passenger plane passes over the Great Plains, and the city of Chicago, making its way to the great port of Boston, one of the birthplaces of American capitalism.

From his office desk in Boston, Mr. Johnson sits on the edge of a $100,000 dollar investment decision while Richard the Moviemaker, 3,000 miles away, waits in silence. Both men are pondering the moment—Johnson contemplating his investment decision and Richard visualizing the airplane trip. This fantasy holds back Richard's anxiety. For Richard to talk now would be an interference with Mr. Johnson's private and personal thoughts. If Richard said anything, it would relieve Richard of his anxiety, but that would destroy the moment, the tension that Mr. Johnson feels so intensely. The mood is heavy.

Johnson: [*Suddenly*] Your papers will be signed and who do you want the check made out to?

Richard: Thank you, partner, and remember we're going to be together for a long, long time. Make the check for $10,000 to MOA Company.

Johnson: I trust you even though we've never met personally. You sound like you know what you're doing.

And with that remark arrangements were made to pick up the check and the papers.

This story is true. Richard Tambor is the moviemaker, and the movie is *Kandyland*, which as of this writing has been successfully completed and is showing in theaters and is available on cassettes at the local video stores. Richard introduced Mr. Johnson's daughter to a theatrical agent and her career is about to get started.

The dialogue has been taken from Richard's diary and the audio tapes he recorded as he made his presentation.

Chapter 13

SALES MEETING ON CLOSING

Question: *What do you do when a prospect who is in a closing frame of mind asks you a question for which you don't have an answer?*

Answer: You say, "Joe, let me research that question for you. I've got an answer in my mind, but I am not sure whether it fits your circumstances fully. I will check it out and call you within an hour."

But that is only a face-saving way out. In my experience a good telephone salesperson, if he has an intelligent prospect, only gets better when he is challenged. My mentor, Bill Abbott, was that way, and taught that to me. It comes with experience.

Question: *You say to begin the closing call with a summation of all the previous calls. Hasn't your prospect forgotten what has occured previously?*

Answer: Of course he has, but even if he has retained only 5 percent or 10 percent of what was said, you have developed his interest. Remember, too, your prospect is human. He has good days and bad days. There is no guarantee that he was up to par when you called. But executives are stable personalities, so there is bound to be continuity in their reactions to you.

Remember that first cold call? You introduced yourself and your company. The advantage of cold calling comes to fruition at the closing stages because you sought him out and he remembers that. If you adhere to the human rules of giving and getting his respect, by informing him of changes in the product price, for instance, and not harassing him needlessly, you have nurtured this prospect to the point of trust, and therefore closing. You built that trust by showing with your actions that you care.

If you mailed him literature and newspaper articles and other interesting things about the product or the industry you are in, you showed your care. How can this person not remember you and the respect and goodwill you showed him? If he remembers you he will remember most or all the conversations you had with him.

Question: *Isn't the selling price the most important thing? If the prospect can buy it a dollar cheaper, won't he?*

Answer: That depends on who you are. Can you offer better service, higher quality? A better company or personal reputation? Can you justify giving the center fielder on one pro baseball team more money than a center fielder on another team? On the surface, you say, "Sure, he's better," and that is the reason he should get more money. But that is only half the story. Suppose the other guy draws more fans to the ball park because he is so well liked? You can get preference over the competition if for some reason you have more to offer.

Question: *You categorize different people such as women, blue collar people, engineers. It almost sounds like Jimmy the Greek talking about breeding athletes.*

Answer: I can see where you could get that impression. I do put groups in different categories based on my experience. But, a common culture can make all the difference in the world. For example, a young Jewish municipal bond broker I know went through the white pages in the Miami telephone directory, calling only what he thought were Jewish last names in elite neighborhoods. If they responded to him in a European accent after he identified himself and his company, he would talk to them in a combination of Yiddish and English. He shared his Jewish culture. I am sure the prospects unconsciously think of the broker as a grandson. They think he is going to take care of them. And he has. He makes a better-than-average living just selling this category of people. He now works on recommendations as well as continuing to canvas.

I will give you another example. A man who worked for me had been trained as an electrical engineer. He asked me to purchase a list of engineers for him to sell. He understood the thinking of engineers very well because he shared that professional culture and, consequently, was very successful in selling them. What would have been difficult or impossible for me was a lot simpler for him.

Question: *Your reference to manipulation, ethical or otherwise— isn't that really a con game?*

Answer: A con man swindles, he tricks, and he abuses. A con man is an unethical manipulator, not a master of persuasion. A con man exploits a situation and totally confuses his sales subject. Richard is a manipulator and a good one because everybody who invested with him gained; they did not lose money. Max hooked into the trusting child in people and the gimmick to get them to call in was the superstar.

Question: *Isn't a movie a fascination to most people, using your metaphor?*

Answer: Sure there was fascination with it, but investing in the movie (even though it was a risky proposition) produced an adult sensation for those who got into it. Let me give you an example that you can understand.

Human beings have many psychological needs and among them are stimuli and structure. Keeping those two needs in mind, let me ask you if you have ever been to the Water Club here in New York City.

Question: *Yes, I have been there. It is a beautiful restaurant. The food is excellent.*

Answer: Now you have answered your own question by the remarks that the food is good and the place is beautifully decorated! The Water Club responds to your hunger, which is stimuli, and the beauty of its dining room is the structure that you need as a human being. You could not say you were conned into eating there, but I assume that the place was recommended to you, wasn't it?

Question: *Yes, it was.*

Answer: So, you were ethically manipulated by the recommendation to go there by a friend whom you trust and the good food that you pictured in your mind before you got there, which served as stimulus, and the structure, the beauty of the dining room. All this combined to give you a good sensation! But suppose the food was lousy and the place was a rat hole and you were told the opposite by your friend. You would have screamed at the top of your lungs that your friend conned you and you would have been right!

Now look at it from another perspective: The food was good, the place decorated nicely, but not up to your standards. Have you been conned? Absolutely not! You haven't been used. It just did not work out for you, but it could have for some one else.

Your friend was trying to be helpful; he meant you no harm. But a con man does mean you harm!

Do you understand the difference now?

Question: *Yes, I do!*

Epilogue

TELEPHONE SELLING IS ALL ABOUT CONFIDENCE

Every business day of the week at least one or two of my salespeople would suddenly "take off" while in a presentation with a prospect. The salesperson's comments after he had successfully closed his deal was "I really felt I was sailing along," or "I got into it heavy," or "I've prospected and I really got into it. I cold called ten good leads." The feeling I always came away with was these salespeople believed in themselves. Because they believed in themselves, they were believable to the prospect. All of us have a certain amount of power. It is in the exploitation of our natural power that we gain our confidence.

To build this confidence you must get on the telephone and work. Certainly there will be mistakes at the beginning; in your timing, in your zeal or over-aggressiveness, and, at times, in your passivity. Sometimes you will mistakenly use the wrong words, or the wrong connotation, or the wrong inflection in your voice.

You must take the responsibility for these mistakes without blaming the prospecting list, the product, the company's selling program, or *your bad luck*. Amplify the bright spots in your presentation at the beginning, and solidify them in your mind by writing them down. Then use them over and over again in all your presentations. Every successful salesperson I've known does this.

As you have seen, successful telephone marketing is hard, sometimes tedious work. It requires much more of you than just dialing the phone. And you cannot be successful by natural instinct alone.

Successful telemarketing calls upon all of your communication abilities. You must control the tone and rhythm of your voice, enunciate clearly, and use words correctly. You must be able to use words, tones, and rhythm to make each prospect see the product in her mind's eye. And you must listen well, because as we have seen, listening is an essential part of effective communication.

But communication abilities are not enough. You must also be psychologically astute so you can "read" your prospect's reactions without any visual help.

You must also understand the consequences of your acts. You need to know how to achieve the sale right way. Many salespeople disagree. They tell me, "What's the difference or why I say things? My method words for me." Working without understanding may be effective in the short run, but it is not the route to lasting success.

You must have a thorough knowledge of your product so you can support your assertions with facts—about your product's construction, its uses, and the like.

And, finally, you must remain as courteous for call number fifty as you are for your first call of the day.

I hope that in reading this book you have come to understand my underlying belief that people, not things, are primary. This belief is a vital part of my success. It can be a vital part of your success too.

GLOSSARY OF TELEPHONE SELLING TERMS

BAIT AND SWITCH   A lower price for higher quality is offered, then switched to something else. This tact is illegal in most states, but still used.

BOILER ROOM   A telephone sales room lacking in selling ethics. Emotional pressure is put on the salespeople to make sales any way they can.

BUCKET SHOP   The same concept as above. The only exception being the product is usually worthless stocks or bonds.

BURNOUT   A tired, listless attitude, usually the result of a salesperson's reaction to rejection by prospects. It could be physical as well as from lack of rest or poor eating habits.

BUZZ WORDS   Those words spoken by the salesperson that seem to prod the prospect into action. Usually these words are metaphors.

CLOSE   The final telephone call when the order is taken for the product or service.

COLD CALLING   The actual physical effort of telephoning the suspect and asking if there is interest in the product or service for sale.

CUE   The recipient of a prospecting call from a telephone salesperson who displays some interest in the product and wants more information.

DROP CLOSE   A situation where the original higher selling price is lowered in order to make a sale.

ETHICAL MANIPULATION   The use of the telephone salesperson's personality to get a certain reaction from a prospect.

FISH   A sucker who buys anything on the first call.

FRONT   A recipient of a prospecting call from a telephone salesperson who displays some interest in the product and wants more information. (Same as a Lead and a Cue)

G   Refers to state, local or federal agency supervising a particular industry of profession.

HARD SELL   A rapid, emotional presentation full of hype and buzz words.

HYPE   Aggressiveness, enthusiasm, and excitement used by the salesperson.

LAY DOWN   A prospect who is all ready to buy with little or no persuasive sales effort on the part of the salesperson. Little or no sales resistance is offered.

LEAD   A recipient of a prospecting call from a telephone salesperson who displays some interest in the product and wants more information. (Same as a front and a cue.)

LOAD   An enlargement of the original order.

ON A DRIVE   A term meaning a salesperson making a hard sell presentation.

PITCH   Giving the sales presentation to the prospect.

PROSPECT   A recipient of a call from a telephone salesperson who has some interest in the item or service for sale.

PROSPECTING   The actual physical effort of telephoning the suspect and seeing if there is interest in the product or service for sale.

QUALIFIED   A prospect that shows some interest and has read all the documents and literature associated with the sale. A qualified prospect or lead will listen to the salesperson's trial close with an open mind.

RELOAD   A repeat order and/or enlarging of the first order.

SOFT SELL   Presentation made on facts and potential use of products or services.

STROKER   A prospect suffering from loneliness who does not want to buy, only talk. An information seeker.

SUSPECT   A name as it appears on a cold calling list that has the right marketing profile.

T.O. (TAKE OVER)   Putting a second salesperson on the phone to close a certain prospect when the first salesperson is close but just cannot seem to do it.

TRIAL CLOSE   The presentation of facts about the item or service for sale.

TROLLING   The actual physical effort of telephoning the suspect and seeing if there is interest in the product or service for sale. (Same as Prospecting)

UNETHICAL MANIPULATION   The same as Ethical Manipulation but devious, asocial behavior is used to get what one wants from a prospect.

INDEX

$14.95

"This book is virtually certain to improve any sales professional's profit margin."

—Robert Rawls, Editor, *Selling Direct*

SUCCESS ON THE LINE

The ABC's of Telephone Selling
Martin M. Novich

It's estimated that nearly ten million people will be selling by telephone in the 1990 s. It's a competitive marketplace, and telephone selling is rarely easy. Whether you are a veteran telephone salesperson or a novice, you want access to the newest information and best thinking on telephone selling.

Success on the Line, by Martin M. Novich, spells out, in down-to-earth terms, new and proven techniques to:

☎ establish rapport quickly and sincerely
☎ influence customers by positive, ethical manipulation
☎ apply sales psychology unique to telemarketing situations
☎ become better attuned to voices—your own and others
☎ build a partnership with customers

Written for freelancers, full-time telephone marketers, and even field sales representatives, *Success on the Line* is packed with examples, sample dialogues, and dos and don'ts lists to reinforce learning. It explores in depth the basics of telephone selling: prospecting and cold call selling. And, Marty Novich goes beyond the usual routines, and shows you how to measurably improve success in this potentially lucrative area.

Selling by telephone is tough and competitive. To survive and prosper, you need at your command a set of highly developed and specialized skills for prospecting, presenting, and closing a sale. It's all here in *Success on the Line*.

MARTIN M. NOVICH is vice president of sales for International Commodity Services in New York City and a contributing editor for the magazine *Selling Direct*.

amacom

American Management Association
135 West 50th Street
New York, NY 10020

ISBN: 0-8144-7725-9

35 235TF1 950
90 24 BR P 4338